ing. Jesus said to His disciples that in the world people will tend
rd it over" other people. But then He says, "Not so with you."
n this "not so with you" spirit that Gary Hoag, Wes Willmer,
Greg Henson have written this extraordinary book, *The Council*.

biblical clarity, *The Council* challenges governance practices
seem to be patterned after the way of this world rather than
wing the Way of Jesus. Hoag, Willmer, and Henson call us back
way of discernment and attending to the voice of the Spirit of
where we are eventually able to declare with authenticity, "It
ed good to the Holy Spirit and to us." *The Council* is a great gift
e church. I haven't found anything in publication that is
tely close to it. This is an important and timely book that is a
-read for all church and Christian ministry boards."

Kent Carlson, Vice President of Leadership Formation,
North American Baptists, Inc.

Council is unmatched in biblical integrity and theological
cation. It's a wonderful resource! Board members everywhere
d use this resource to gain a biblical mindset, a descriptive
l, and a practical map for board service. I plan to share it
y in the USA, South Korea, and around the world."

Sung Wook Chung, DPhil (Oxford University),
ssor of Christian Theology and Director of Asian Initiatives,
Denver Seminary; Board President, Kurios International

book articulates what's been ruminating in my heart about
governance for over 25 years! It's a 'must-read' for every believer
erves in a board capacity and a 'go-to resource' for board chairs
hose who lead board development. Thank you, gentlemen!"

Holly Culhane, Founder/CEO, Presence Point, Inc.;
Board Vice Chair, Youth for Christ USA; Board Member and
ard Development Chair, Evangelical Christian Credit Union

fight
to "l
It is
and

Witl
that
follo
to a
God
seen
to tl
rem(
mus

"*The
appli
shou
mod
wide

Pro

"This
board
who
and t

B(

"Calling for renewed approaches related to board governance for Christian entities and organizations, *The Council* provides biblically-grounded counsel, informed by key insights from tradition, to offer fresh direction and faithful principles for oversight in churches, as well as church-related institutions and organizations. Gary Hoag, Wes Willmer, and Greg Henson are to be congratulated for helping board members, overseers, and administrators think more intentionally, purposefully, and Christianly about this important work. It is a privilege to recommend this book with the hope that it will help all of us as we seek to steward wisely and govern faithfully the various institutions and entities that we serve."

David S. Dockery, Ph.D., President, Trinity International University / Trinity Evangelical Divinity School; President, Evangelical Theological Society

"We are called to serve as responsible stewards and faithful administrators of God's resources entrusted to us. Those who oversee God's work need wisdom and humility to do it God's way. Hoag, Willmer, and Henson clearly articulate the biblical insights that overseers need to know in *The Council* in a manner that is both understandable and globally applicable. Thank you, dear brothers."

Angelito M. Gabriel, FICD, Trustee and Treasurer, Mission Aviation Fellowship Philippines; Executive Director, Christian Council for Accountability and Transparency

"*The Council* is very relevant for any ministry today. Too often we overlook biblical texts which are able to give us perspective on how to manage and govern as faithful stewards in God's mission. I highly recommend this book to board members and ministry administrators wanting to learn more about how God wants us to establish better governance practices. It should be required reading for any new board member too. Thank you for putting this resource in the hands of the Church!"

"I thoroughly enjoyed reading this book because I could identify with the disconnect between practice and Scripture that I have encountered in over 25 years of governance in Christian organizations and churches. The recommended practical tools are deeply soul searching and are gems for organizational discipleship. I highly recommend this book so that we can 'Walk the Word' in governance."

"As a Christian nonprofit board member and steward, I celebrate this book! Impressive! In only about 100 pages, I found the answers I have longed for after 25 years of service on American and Latino nonprofit boards. In Guatemala and across Latin America, most of the training for boards comes only from the business world which usually centers around money, pride, control, and status. This book opens our eyes and equips us to do governance in a Christian way."

"How inspiring to read this deep and enriching biblical study about board governance. Together as Christian board members, we learn from the Scriptures how to let the Holy Spirit lead us, so that we work in unison. We are not the owners of God's work, but stewards who now understand our role as overseers."

"With the abundance of books on board governance, none of them are as deeply rooted in God's design for oversight than *The Council*. This book is for anyone who seeks diligently to steward nonprofit organizations with God-honoring excellence. It provides the ultimate biblical framework for readers who are wholeheartedly committed to pursuing the Kingdom path agenda for their organizations."

Tami Heim, President & CEO, Christian Leadership Alliance

"Through this book Gary, Wes, and Greg have made a significant contribution to the literature on Christian governance. It moves seamlessly from scholarly exegesis to biblical themes to practical advice and descriptions of why and how Christian governance must be different from secular governance. For many boards and church councils, this book will be the paradigm shift they need to re-energise their oversight."

Steve Kerr, Executive Director, CMA Standards Council;
Board Member, Overseas Council Australia

"I have been waiting for a book like *The Council* for over twenty years. Fortunately, Hoag, Willmer, and Henson have made it worth my wait. All three men are scholars and practitioners in their diverse areas. They are also churchmen who know board governance. *The Council* is chock-full of exegetical, historical, and pastoral insights. Apply the wisdom of this book and your board and administrative teams will thank you, and they will never be the same."

Keith R. Krell, Ph.D., Senior Pastor & Elder Chair,
Fourth Memorial Church, Spokane, WA

"With a creative use of the councils in the Bible and the Church as an example, this book gives spiritual guidance applicable for all boards. It lays down clear spiritual boundaries for helping boards govern more effectively. I highly recommend this book to all."

P. K. D. Lee, Board Member, Powerhouse Church, Tambaram, India; Executive Committee Member, Lausanne Ministry Fundraising Network

"*The Council* gives a vital insight into what the Bible says about board governance. This text researches and highlights the imperatives of the biblical governance characteristics whilst carefully showing the snares and pitfalls to be avoided. Thank you to Gary, Wesley, and Gregory for this important tool."

Jame Lewis, Llb B.Comm., Chair, Eastern College Australia; Board Member, Christian Ministry Advancement and Hillcrest Christian College; Hon Lawyer, Baptist Union of Victoria

"*The Council* is an inspiring guide with great challenges to those serving in governance ministry. It is good to understand governance is a God-breathed and blessed vocation and essential that we first bring God's Word to the table inviting the Holy Spirit into our meetings to speak through Scripture, Standing in Silence, Sharing, and Supplication."

René E. Palacio, SIM International Director of Governance

"Governance is a complex subject and generally, not much material is available on this issue. Linking governance to the biblical model requires a thorough understanding of the Word of God and a glimpse of God's heart. Gary G. Hoag, Wesley K. Willmer, and Gregory J. Henson have authored the book, *The Council*, which captures very well the issue of governance for the Christian context. Throughout the book, they explain the four warning signals for governance and what to do to overcome them. It is a highly commendable effort and a 'must-read' book for people charged with governance."

Sanjay Patra, FCA, Ph.D., Executive Director, Financial Management Service Foundation; Board Chair, Evangelical Financial Accountability Council, New Delhi, India.

"Thank you to the authors for this timeless reminder of the biblical truths of what constitutes good governance. Not only does the book provide helpful hints on how boards can improve their alignment with God's will, but also provides warnings about some of the temptations that can steer boards away from the way God would want us to apply governance principles."

John Peberdy, Chairman, Christian Ministry Advancement (CMA), Australia

"Good governance is a critical element of performance, impact, and health in any organisation. It requires a strong blend of professionalism from the head and passion from the heart, deeply grounded in prayer and discernment. In the current climate it is more important than ever that directors are well equipped with the capabilities and insights to govern well. This book is a timely and valuable resource, providing wisdom and a perspective on what the Bible says about governance (which is actually quite a lot!). I highly commend it to any current boards or aspiring directors."

Ross Piper, CEO, Christian Super; Board Member, Brightlight Impact Advisory and Investment Management; Responsible Impact Association of Australia; Board Member, SEED

"Important, intentional, strategic, and transformative! This insightful and refreshing treatise biblically reframes much contemporary Christian governance practice. Does your governing board or council exhibit the characteristics embodied in the 20 hard questions in chapter 7? If you serve in governance you definitely need this book!"

Allan Priest, Director and Deputy Chair of both Baptist Financial Services Australia Ltd and Baptist Care (South Australia) Foundation Nominees Pty Ltd as trustee for Baptist Care (South Australia) Foundation; Past President, Baptist Churches of South Australia; Former Chair, Baptist Care (South Australia) and Rostrevor Baptist Church

"Few books give a biblical framework for governance. The authors have succeeded in developing a simple biblical schema that informs the workings of the board. It is a practical book that many will find useful as they seek to serve God on Christian nonprofit boards."

Dr. R. J. Rawson OAM, Chair, Power to Change (Cru Australia) and Global Aid Network (Australia); Board Member, Christian Ministry Advancement (CMA), Australia; Former CEO, Scripture Union Queensland

"The thought of reading a book on board governance scared me. So many leadership teams have fallen into a reliance on their own abilities. But having read *The Council*, I could not have been more surprised. This is a book that all leadership teams need to read in order to keep in step with the Spirit and to begin to discern where God is leading His people to join Him on mission. Not only will I get copies for my own team of elders, I will recommend this book in each of my seminary classes, through the Forge International Network, and to every church in my denomination."

Dr. Cameron Roxburgh, VP of Missional Initiatives, North American Baptists, Inc.; National Director, Forge Canada; Senior Pastor, Southside Community Church

"*The Council* offers more than just a practical exegesis of biblical texts. It provides a new set of spectacles through which your heart and mind can assess your own performance. I expect this book will breathe new life and understanding into future expressions of Christian governance."

Barbara Shantz, Co-leader, Lausanne Ministry Fundraising Network

"*The Council* brings to life images of biblical discernment and decision making. The authors do not propose a three-step quick fix, rather they ask the reader to wrestle with the text and apply a biblical perspective to their local organisational context. This book is a breath of fresh air in a field so often dominated by management theory dressed up as Christian governance."

Stephen Smith, Principal & Associate Professor,
The Australian College of Ministries

"Gary Hoag, as always, gives me deeper and better advice than I would think to ask for. With the help of Wesley Willmer and Gregory Henson, they challenge me to examine the undergirding characteristics of a godly board—one whose decisions are made, not through human grids, but through a scriptural grid. Like *The Sower* and *The Choice*, the reader is given tools of evaluation through the lens of the Kingdom path rather than a common path. Thanks ECFAPress for a gem for governance."

Bob Snyder, M.D., President and Board Member, IHS Global

"*The Council* is excellent guide on approaching board governance from a Christian perspective, mixing biblical examination with practical advice. I was inspired to rethink governance from the ground up, rather than trying to tweak existing secular governance principles."

Raewyn Williams, Conference President,
Churches of Christ NSW, Australia

"Seldom is a book both timely and timeless, but *The Council* pushes into this rare territory. Using biblical history along with transparent and practical insights, the text informs and inspires those who desire to wisely steward a godly mission. Prepare to be moved. Prepare to be challenged. I was."

Dan Wolgemuth, President/CEO, Youth for Christ

THE
COUNCIL

A Biblical Perspective on
Board Governance

Gary G. Hoag, Wesley K. Willmer, &
Gregory J. Henson

ECFA.org/ECFAPress.aspx

Cover: *Café Terrace at Night*, Vincent Van Gogh

Scripture quotations are from the New International Version of the Bible (NIV) unless otherwise noted.

Copyright © 2018 ECFAPress

ISBN: 978-1-936233-94-6

Table of Contents

Foreword

Where can I go to get biblical advice on board governance? This often-asked question has puzzled board members for decades. *The Council* answers this question by starting with the Scriptures and ending with the Scriptures.

Thanks to the deep dive that Hoag, Willmer, and Henson take into the Scriptures, the question has now been more fully answered than ever before. That is a strong statement, but I am convinced it is true. The authors take the reader on a journey back through the pages of time, stepping right into the biblical record of four key councils which now stand as enduring examples to us – in some cases giving us a model to emulate, and in others offering a lesson in pitfalls to avoid. The second half of the book pulls the insights from the biblical texts together into practical, actionable applications to refine our thinking and define our steps.

This book is outstanding for five reasons which rarely apply to a book:

1. **Universal.** This book applies to a broad spectrum of organizations. It is relevant for Christ-centered churches and other nonprofit ministries. It contains essential truths pertaining to organizations both large and small. *The Council* universally applies across denominational lines, and is appropriate for churches whether denominational or independent. The book has universal application regardless

of country or locality. As governance is one of the three priorities of ECFA, along with faithful administration of finances and resource development, we are thrilled to publish this book at ECFAPress for universal application.

2. **Transformative.** The principles embodied in *The Council* hold the potential to change the governance practices and outcomes for all Christ-centered churches and nonprofit ministries. Every board can fine-tune their operations even if the board is healthy. *The Council* has the potential to enhance the trajectory of every board.

3. **Timeless.** *The Council* is a principle-based text that will apply as much in the future as it does today. We are reminded of the parable of the wise and foolish builders in Matthew chapter 7. Jesus taught the disciples through this parable, saying, "Everyone who hears these words of mine and puts them into practice is like a wise man who built his house on the rock." The authors of *The Council* have wisely built this study of biblical board governance on a solid foundation of scriptural truth that is unchanging regardless of culture or circumstance. After you read this book, you will be drawn back to it over and over as you desire to refresh your biblically based mindset on board governance.

4. **Practical.** The twenty questions in chapter 7 provide an excellent road map for boards to implement the principles in the book. Additionally, the study guide is designed to help overseers deepen their biblical knowledge and perspective on board governance.

5. **Inspiring.** Other authors have also urged prayer, the reading of Scripture during board meetings, setting aside time for silence, and welcoming all board members to share their thoughts. But *The Council* is unmistakably clear in presenting the biblical rationale for engaging in these practices and sets them forth in a refreshing and inspiring way.

As I read *The Council*, the Holy Spirit stirred my soul and gave me a vision of how this book will inspire boards of Christ-centered churches and ministries to improve their biblical mindset for their governance work. Father, may it be so!

"Therefore everyone who hears these words of mine and puts them into practice is like a wise man who built his house on the rock" (Matthew 7:24).

Dan Busby
President
ECFA

Preface

"It seemed good to the Holy Spirit and to us…"

I think the retrieval of these words from Acts 15:28 is my favorite part of this book! It is a salutary reminder that when we come together as Christians, our foremost concern should be to seek God's will.

This emphasis reminded me of a meeting I was part of about two decades ago. I've been in a lot of meetings since, but something about this one has stuck in my mind. It was a task force for a new venture, and one of the participants suggested devoting some of our time together in prayer. The chair responded that we pray individually at home and (besides opening and closing in prayer), we come together to discuss. The inference was that we didn't want to waste our time together praying. So we didn't. But we certainly missed an opportunity, and I don't think our experience is unique. How different things would be if we understood seeking God corporately as central to our purpose rather than a distraction from the main game. The hymn, "What a Friend We Have in Jesus," says in part:

> O what peace we often forfeit,
>
> O what needless pain we bear,
>
> All because we do not carry
>
> Everything to God in prayer!

How many futile board meetings have there been, how much aimless discussion, how many unhelpful disputes, all because everyone was speaking out of their own limited imaginations rather than accessing the wisdom of Christ? Godly wisdom often involves seeing a third way between two competing options, as Solomon's famous verdict on the two women demonstrates. This is the wisdom that God promises to those who ask—a promise I value all the more with every passing year.

Of course, this means that when appointing board members we need to consider not only their technical expertise, but also their spiritual maturity—that they know what it means to seek God. Sometimes people who have been very successful in secular business can be a wonderful asset to Christian boards. But sometimes they have unquestioningly adopted the world's definition of success and, confident in their own ability, see no need to rely on God. Paul's admonition not to be conformed to the pattern of this world, but rather transformed by the renewing of our minds, is a constant challenge to all of us.

By taking us back to the sources in Scripture and the early church, Gary, Wesley, and Gregory have made a welcome and important contribution to Christian governance. If we take what they say seriously, we will avoid becoming blind guides who adhere to procedures and frameworks, but neglect the weightier matters of justice, mercy, and faith.

Edwina Murphy, Ph.D.
Morling College, Sydney, Australia

Introduction

"What does the Bible say about board governance?"

Among common answers, a few people exclaim with more than a hint of frustration, "Not enough!" Some people cite passages in Proverbs that offer timeless wisdom. Others mention New Testament texts in which the apostle Paul sets forth character qualifications for overseers.

Many answer the question with more questions, saying, "What kind of board? Are you referring to a church board, a Christian ministry board, a secular nonprofit board, a corporate board, a municipal or government board, or some other board?"

Should it matter? Think about it. If we are followers of Jesus Christ, should our approach to governance on the homeowners association board on which we show our love for our neighbors differ when compared to our service on a Christ-centered rescue mission board or even a local church board? Of course, government laws and statutes have different legal requirements for these various boards, but that's neither the topic in view nor what this book is about.

We wrote this book to answer the question, "What does the Bible say about board governance?" because we believe that followers of Jesus Christ who serve in board governance settings must start with the Scriptures. We must understand and adopt a biblically based mindset to position our Christian faith to inform and transform our thinking on oversight, just like it shapes every other aspect of life.

Consequently, we searched the Scriptures and studied the governing bodies or "councils" that appear in the biblical record. We found four of them. Our analysis of the four councils appears in the first four chapters. Interestingly, the four councils offer keen insight regarding how to think about governance and how not to think about it. Then the last three chapters present the mindset or biblical framework that comes into view, a model of spiritual disciplines for maintaining the biblical mindset, and a map that suggests a sound starting point and hard questions to help readers find their way.

We pray the timeless, transcultural, and biblical perspective set forth in this book transforms your thinking about board governance and impacts the trajectory of every council on which you serve for God's glory.

> "It seemed good to the Holy Spirit and to us not to burden you with anything beyond the following requirements" (Acts 15:28).

Gary G. Hoag, Ph.D.
Wesley K. Willmer, Ph.D.
Gregory J. Henson, M.B.A.

Chapter One

The Council of Moses

*"The task of the elders will be to help in the administration
of the immense population, in its varied needs, especially in the context
of the increasing impiety of the people."[1]*
Ronald B. Allen

The appointment of elders to govern people goes back to the oldest portions of Scripture. Largely speaking, the energy of such groups in antiquity focused on the oversight of communities. In plain terms, people misbehaved, and councils helped them maintain order and settle disputes.

This chapter looks at the first council in the biblical record, the Council of Moses. In Numbers 11 we find a foundational paradigm for thinking biblically about governance. This analysis aims not at revealing the practical aspects of oversight but rather the mindset and posture God desires for overseers.

Numbers 11 – The Formation of the Council

> *"Some seventy elders are to be given some of Moses'*
> *spirit and thereby enabled to share his burdens with him.*
> *Since his administrative duties were already shared with others,*
> *these elders must have been intended to give*
> *him spiritual support."*[2]
> Gordon Wenham

Three days after God miraculously delivered His people from Pharaoh through the Red Sea, they complained to Moses about the lack of food and water. In response, God faithfully provided for them (cf. Exodus 15:22–27).

One year later and just three days into their march to the Promised Land, God's people complained to Moses again. Let us grasp the magnitude of the grumbling: the people numbered 600,000 men plus women and children, so this was no small group of naysayers.

This brief historical sketch sets the stage for reading Numbers 11. In this text we find the formation of the Council of Moses and specific biblical insights related to governance.

> [1] Now the people complained about their hardships in the hearing of the Lord, and when he heard them his anger was aroused. Then fire from the Lord burned among them and consumed some of the outskirts of the camp. [2] When the people cried out to Moses, he prayed to the Lord and the fire died down. [3] So that place was called Taberah, because fire from the Lord had burned among them.
>
> [4] The rabble with them began to crave other food, and again the Israelites started wailing and said, "If only we had meat

to eat! ⁵ We remember the fish we ate in Egypt at no cost—also the cucumbers, melons, leeks, onions and garlic. ⁶ But now we have lost our appetite; we never see anything but this manna!"

⁷ The manna was like coriander seed and looked like resin. ⁸ The people went around gathering it, and then ground it in a hand mill or crushed it in a mortar. They cooked it in a pot or made it into loaves. And it tasted like something made with olive oil. ⁹ When the dew settled on the camp at night, the manna also came down.

¹⁰ Moses heard the people of every family wailing at the entrance to their tents. The Lord became exceedingly angry, and Moses was troubled. ¹¹ He asked the Lord, "Why have you brought this trouble on your servant? What have I done to displease you that you put the burden of all these people on me? ¹² Did I conceive all these people? Did I give them birth? Why do you tell me to carry them in my arms, as a nurse carries an infant, to the land you promised on oath to their ancestors? ¹³ Where can I get meat for all these people? They keep wailing to me, 'Give us meat to eat!' ¹⁴ I cannot carry all these people by myself; the burden is too heavy for me. ¹⁵ If this is how you are going to treat me, please go ahead and kill me—if I have found favor in your eyes—and do not let me face my own ruin."

¹⁶ The Lord said to Moses: "Bring me seventy of Israel's elders who are known to you as leaders and officials among the people. Have them come to the tent of meeting, that they may stand there with you. ¹⁷ I will come down and speak with you there, and I will take some of the power of the Spirit

that is on you and put it on them. They will share the burden of the people with you so that you will not have to carry it alone."

[18] "Tell the people: 'Consecrate yourselves in preparation for tomorrow, when you will eat meat. The Lord heard you when you wailed, "If only we had meat to eat! We were better off in Egypt!" Now the Lord will give you meat, and you will eat it. [19] You will not eat it for just one day, or two days, or five, ten or twenty days, [20] but for a whole month—until it comes out of your nostrils and you loathe it—because you have rejected the Lord, who is among you, and have wailed before him, saying, "Why did we ever leave Egypt?"'"

[21] But Moses said, "Here I am among six hundred thousand men on foot, and you say, 'I will give them meat to eat for a whole month!' [22] Would they have enough if flocks and herds were slaughtered for them? Would they have enough if all the fish in the sea were caught for them?"

[23] The Lord answered Moses, "Is the Lord's arm too short? Now you will see whether or not what I say will come true for you."

[24] So Moses went out and told the people what the Lord had said. He brought together seventy of their elders and had them stand around the tent. [25] Then the Lord came down in the cloud and spoke with him, and he took some of the power of the Spirit that was on him and put it on the seventy elders. When the Spirit rested on them, they prophesied—but did not do so again.

²⁶ However, two men, whose names were Eldad and Medad, had remained in the camp. They were listed among the elders, but did not go out to the tent. Yet the Spirit also rested on them, and they prophesied in the camp. ²⁷ A young man ran and told Moses, "Eldad and Medad are prophesying in the camp."

²⁸ Joshua son of Nun, who had been Moses' aide since youth, spoke up and said, "Moses, my lord, stop them!"

²⁹ But Moses replied, "Are you jealous for my sake? I wish that all the Lord's people were prophets and that the Lord would put his Spirit on them!" ³⁰ Then Moses and the elders of Israel returned to the camp.

³¹ Now a wind went out from the Lord and drove quail in from the sea. It scattered them up to two cubits deep all around the camp, as far as a day's walk in any direction. ³² All that day and night and all the next day the people went out and gathered quail. No one gathered less than ten homers. Then they spread them out all around the camp. ³³ But while the meat was still between their teeth and before it could be consumed, the anger of the Lord burned against the people, and he struck them with a severe plague. ³⁴ Therefore the place was named Kibroth Hattaavah, because there they buried the people who had craved other food.

³⁵ From Kibroth Hattaavah the people traveled to Hazeroth and stayed there.

God's people were tired of eating manna. They craved the variety of food they enjoyed back in Egypt (Numbers 11:1–9). Moses, weary from their complaining, poured out his heart to the Lord in anguish (Numbers 11:10–15). From his viewpoint, the need was greater than all their flocks and herds as well as all of the proverbial fish in the sea. Overwhelmed by the situation, Moses was ready to throw in the towel. He wanted to give up!

Have you been there? Most pastors and ministry administrators can relate to the depth of his anguish. It's that frustrating feeling when it seems like everyone is murmuring as order unravels around you.

The Lord responded to the situation with instructions for Moses to appoint a council and to get ready for lots of meat (Numbers 11:16–17). Though many translations describe the candidates for oversight as, "leaders and officials," perhaps a clarified definition for this group comes through the NASB rendering, "elders of the people and their officials."

These terms imply that Moses must locate seventy servants who are seasoned "elders," which points to experience and maturity, along with "officials" who may be younger but exhibit proven skill and administrative gifting. These "elders of the people and their officials" must *not* see themselves as leaders *per se*; instead, they govern affairs and help the people follow God as their Leader.[3]

The seventy were to assemble at the tent of meeting, which was the place where the Lord met with Moses. Their job was to stand and listen there with Moses. Standing before God acknowledges God's rule and portrays a posture of service for sharing the burden of the people, and the location for their standing inferred that the capacity to execute this service would come from the Lord. Additionally, each elder would receive the power of the Spirit and prophesy as a sign of empowerment.

Before Moses departed to form the council, the Lord alerted him that so much meat would come the next day that people would eat it for a month (Numbers 11:18–23). Moses could not even dream of that much meat after one year of a steady diet of manna, manna, and more manna. They would become sick!

Sound familiar? Rather than judge these whiners, most of us can relate to this situation in our contemporary settings. We recall times when a governing body chose a different path than one of dependence on God. We remember these situations vividly because of the terrible consequences that resulted from them!

Back in the narrative, two elders, Eldad and Medad, had gone rogue (Numbers 11:24–30). They were not prophesying at the tent of meeting as instructed but were out in the camp. Moses learned of this from his trustworthy aid, Joshua, and keenly averted a possible conflict in the camp by saying that he wished all of God's people had the Spirit on them.

Ever wish you could think that fast and profoundly? Joshua saw the situation as a problem. Moses saw it as an opportunity to proclaim his hope to see the Spirit at work in the lives of all of God's people! Certainly, it appears that Eldad and Medad had not followed the specific commission from the Lord to stand with God's servant at the tent of meeting. The response of Moses, however, inspires future servants like us not to react negatively to the unexpected behavior of elders, but to respond in a way that celebrates the direction we discern the Lord is moving His people.

Returning to the story, the situation unfolded just as the Lord had said. Meat arrived in the form of quail two cubits deep. As the Lord had said, a plague spread among the people. Many died. After burying the people, they named the place to remind them of what happened there (Numbers 11:31–35). This was a common practice in antiquity to ensure that the people remembered the lessons learned in particular places.

By including this account in the fourth book of the Law, Moses passed on this lesson to all God's people after him. It reveals God's heart on oversight, and helps us form a governance paradigm with four distinct characteristics.

Four Characteristics of the Council of Moses

While many insights surface when examining the Council of Moses, four characteristics emerge as significant in describing how the council should approach the oversight of God's people. This section summarizes the four traits that surface in two central verses of this text, Numbers 11:16–17.

> [16] The Lord said to Moses: "Bring me seventy of Israel's elders who are known to you as leaders and officials among the people. Have them come to the tent of meeting, that they may stand there with you. [17] I will come down and speak with you there, and I will take some of the power of the Spirit that is on you and put it on them. They will share the burden of the people with you so that you will not have to carry it alone."

1. Spiritual Maturity and Administrative Gifting

The Lord instructed Moses to bring seventy "leaders and officials" (NIV), or more precisely, "elders of the people and their officials" (NASB), to help him govern. Again, the term "elders" points to servants with proven experience and spiritual maturity, and "their officials" implies candidates of any age that exhibit administrative gifting among the people.

Moses was not to identify them and then lead, as that was God's job. The Lord told him to bring these seventy elders to Him. This reveals that their service would submit to God's rule. It also connotes that the Lord wanted these overseers to know Him deeply, so that their service reflected His heart, and so His guidance would shape their governance.

While we do not know for certain about the background of the seventy, they probably would have been known to Moses, having served among the people, and may have numbered among the "officials" that had been appointed at the suggestion of Jethro, the father-in-law of Moses, as recounted in Exodus 18:19–23.

> [19] Listen now to me and I will give you some advice, and may God be with you. You must be the people's representative before God and bring their disputes to him. [20] Teach them his decrees and instructions, and show them the way they are to live and how they are to behave. [21] But select capable men from all the people—men who fear God, trustworthy men who hate dishonest gain—and appoint them as officials over thousands, hundreds, fifties and tens. [22] Have them serve as judges for the people at all times, but have them bring every difficult case to you; the simple cases they can

decide themselves. That will make your load lighter, because they will share it with you. [23] If you do this and God so commands, you will be able to stand the strain, and all these people will go home satisfied.

Jethro advised Moses to get help to handle the administration of the people. He must find God-fearing, trustworthy servants who hate dishonest gain and teach them everything they need to know. Their heavy lifting would lighten his load. So, while we cannot locate with certainty the identity of the "elders" and "officials" that Moses chose in Numbers 11, we suggest that some likely came from this experienced group of willing servants who would have been known to Moses.

As we begin to think about oversight in churches and ministries, this biblical example points us to look for mature elders and gifted administrators as candidates. We would do well to look for God-fearing, trustworthy servants who hate dishonest gain. Such character traits position servants to govern God's work under God's rule.

2. Standing and Listening Posture

Once appointed and brought to the Lord, the council assumes a specific posture in a certain place with Moses. They must come and stand at the tent of meeting with God's servant. The tent of meeting was the place where the Lord met with people. It was a place of listening and divine communion.

The standing posture reflects attentiveness to hear from the Lord and submission to His rule. Remember, they were God's chosen people! By both standing and listening in this place, we can deduce that it would unify them and cause them to govern in a godly way in the direction that matched the desires of the Lord. For a possible picture of this intimate relationship with God, consider this striking scene recounted in Exodus 24:9–11.

> [9] Moses and Aaron, Nadab and Abihu, and the seventy elders of Israel went up [10] and saw the God of Israel. Under his feet was something like a pavement made of lapis lazuli, as bright blue as the sky. [11] But God did not raise His hand against these leaders of the Israelites; they saw God, and they ate and drank.

In this instance, standing and listening puts Moses, Aaron, Nadab, Abihu, and the seventy in position to get an invitation from God to come up, to see Him, and to experience deeper communion with Him. This closeness is depicted by the beautiful picture of eating and drinking together.

For clarity, the "leaders of the Israelites" appears as "nobles of the sons of Israel" in the NASB, which is another expression used to describe the elders and officials. We put forth this point to remind readers that God is the "Leader" of His people, while the elders and officials stand and govern under His authority.

Imagine standing and listening as a governing board. It would not be a new practice. Throughout church history, we find many instances of standing during the reading of Scripture coupled with silence to hear from God. Many churches and ministries still do this. Visualize the potential impact of taking the posture of standing and listening in governance settings to remind overseers to submit to and govern on behalf of God as the Leader!

3. The Presence and Power of the Spirit

A third trait of the Council of Moses reflects its source of power and unity. The Lord spreads the same Spirit on the council members that is on Moses. Mystical manifestations like this are rare in the Old Testament. They authenticate that God is at work. In another instance with Moses recounted in Exodus 31:1–5, the Spirit of God empowers Bezalel to do great things.

> [1] Then the Lord said to Moses, [2] "See, I have chosen Bezalel son of Uri, the son of Hur, of the tribe of Judah, [3] and I have filled him with the Spirit of God, with wisdom, with understanding, with knowledge and with all kinds of skills — [4] to make artistic designs for work in gold, silver and bronze, [5] to cut and set stones, to work in wood, and to engage in all kinds of crafts.

Anyone in governance settings, such as the seventy of the Council of Moses or overseers today, may be tempted to rely on human might and wisdom, or "the flesh" as described in other biblical texts, rather than the Spirit. We must intentionally avoid this tendency. Simultaneously, the elders must not work to create unity but rather to preserve the unity they already have. The text states that the Lord would spread the Spirit around. So, it is God who unifies the seventy with the Spirit as they stand together.

Back in Numbers 11, however, Eldad and Medad did not go to the tent of meeting as directed but remained in the camp, and the Spirit still rested on them. This teaches that the Spirit can still work through people who do not follow instructions. That's comforting news! Nevertheless, overseers must set an example by serving in obedience to God.

4. Humble Service

The final characteristic of the Council of Moses shows that the council members got their proverbial hands dirty as humble servants. Their function was to share the burden of the people with God's servant, Moses. He was weary and the job was too big as his own words reveal when speaking about God's people in Deuteronomy 1:9-12.

> [9] At that time I said to you, "You are too heavy a burden for me to carry alone. [10] The Lord your God has increased your numbers so that today you are as numerous as the stars in the sky. [11] May the Lord, the God of your ancestors, increase you a thousand times and bless you as he has promised! [12] But how can I bear your problems and your burdens and your disputes all by myself?"

To share Moses' burdens meant the seventy would voluntarily inconvenience themselves and put the needs of the people ahead of their own. They would help solve disputes, which would have been messy and likely called for patience to deal with frustrating people and situations.

Governance God's way requires humble service. The administration of the Lord's work is hard, and the governance becomes even more complex as the overseers have to come alongside God's appointed servant to help sort out the messes. People get derailed, and overseers help them get back on track and stay there.

Summary

The Council of Moses provides a foundational paradigm for thinking biblically about board governance. Four characteristics come into view in Numbers 11 that show us what the Lord desires for overseers. They represent elders and officials with proven spiritual maturity and demonstrated administrative gifting. They stand with God's appointed servant in a place where they can hear from the Lord. The Spirit of God empowers and unifies them. Lastly, they aid God's servants in sharing the burden of the people as humble servants. We can trace this council in the biblical record for more than a thousand years into New Testament times.

Chapter Two

The Jewish Council
in the First Century

"The Jerusalem Sanhedrin's sphere of authority
extended over the spiritual, political, and legal affairs of the Jews."[4]
Graham H. Twelftree

More than a millennium after Moses, the Jewish Council still incorporated a high priest plus seventy members, but that may be where the comparison ends. While the form of the Council of Moses prevailed, we find the function shifted considerably by the days of Jesus. In short, they moved from governing under God's rule to serving as the "ruling council" (John 3:1).

Scholars locate the power swing during the Maccabean period (second century B.C.) in which the Jewish Council becomes known as the "Sanhedrin." The name means, "sitting together." Notice the blatant posture change in contrast to the standing Council of Moses! Most biblical references to the Sanhedrin translate the term simply as "assembly" or "council." The Sanhedrin interfaced with Rome to rule over the Jews.

John 11:47–50 – The Function of the Sanhedrin

"In antiquity, every community gathered together
its leading members to bring leadership and order to civic life.
Jerusalem had its own lay nobility — men who were
keenly invested in the success of Jerusalem and
who worked closely with the temple priests to bring order...
These elders joined together with select members
of the priesthood (who were generally Sadducees) and
leading Pharisees to form a "high council" called the Sanhedrin."[5]
Gary M. Burge

By the first century A.D., we find that the composition of the Sanhedrin had changed. In addition to "elders and officials" with spiritual maturity and administrative gifting like we see in the Council of Moses, the group also includes well-educated legal experts who cared deeply about preserving Jewish rules and traditions and religious leaders who had attained their posts linked to their lineage, wealth, and status.

The Mishnah reports the existence of lesser councils or lower courts with twenty-three members and the high priest to judge intermediate cases (cf. Mishnah, *Sanh.* 1.6). Candidates for these councils were picked from householders. Again, this implies some measure of wealth and status. The Sanhedrin ruled the people like a full governing board, and the lesser courts appear as task forces to handle more minor matters. Jewish communities outside Jerusalem had similar structures in local synagogues.

We read about the Sanhedrin in various texts in the Gospels where it emerges as the nefarious nocturnal assembly that put Jesus on trial (cf. Matthew 26:59; Mark 15:1; Luke 22:66; John 11:47) and the group that tried to stifle the ministry of the apostles who labored to advance the gospel (cf. Acts 5:27).

John 11:47–50 illustrates how the high priest, the chief priest, and the Pharisees functioned as rulers in Jerusalem. This text reports excerpts of the meeting of the Sanhedrin immediately after the account of Jesus raising Lazarus from the dead. Caiaphas, who assumed the chair from his father-in-law, Annas (which also illustrates how power passed through family lines) led the assembly.

[47] Then the chief priests and the Pharisees called a meeting of the Sanhedrin. "What are we accomplishing?" they asked. "Here is this man performing many signs. [48] If we let him go on like this, everyone will believe in him, and then the Romans will come and take away both our temple and our nation." [49] Then one of them, named Caiaphas, who was high priest that year, spoke up, "You know nothing at all! [50] You do not realize that it is better for you that one man die for the people than that the whole nation perish."

The guiding voice of the Council of Moses was the Word of the Lord, but by the first century, the Sanhedrin appears to follow the guidance of the high priest, Caiaphas. While our knowledge of this and other Sanhedrin meetings is limited, we have no biblical record that the Scriptures influenced the proceedings of the Sanhedrin.

Ever been in a meeting where the overseers appear to have shifted from governing to talking and acting like they owned the place? Any time a group of people wields spiritual, political, and legal authority, it puts everyone around them in a dangerous position. What made this group even more grievous is that their oral interpretation of Torah had become encrusted tradition; the people were expected to observe it as law.

We can trace the shift in power from governing to ruling to at least two major factors that took place just after the Maccabean revolt. The authority of the high priest position swelled when Simon Maccabeus was appointed high priest, military chief, and ethnarch (political leader) of the Jews (c. 140 B.C.). Also, during the reign of Queen Alexandra (76–67 B.C.), the power of the Sanhedrin grew when the group became dominated by the Pharisees rather than priests or other elders.[6] The people had to follow their wishes and understanding of Torah, or else!

What can boards do to ensure they don't shift from governing to ruling? We suggest that identifying the snares that overtook the Sanhedrin can help overseers avoid such sinister traps and maintain a biblical perspective on board governance.

Four Snares of the Sanhedrin

The Sanhedrin drifted from the pattern of the Council of Moses both in the composition of the seventy and its function in relation to the people in at least four ways. We identify them as four snares. They come together to form a recipe for disaster.

1. Selecting People of Status

By the days of Jesus, the Sanhedrin likely still included elders and officials of proven spiritual maturity and demonstrated administrative gifting like the Council of Moses, but others had infiltrated the ranks. These candidates were often chosen from a pool of householders, which brings some measure of wealth into view as a factor for appointment. Specifically, we find two sets of people of status—chief priests and Pharisees.

Leading or chief priests, often Sadducees, would have been experts in the Torah, the written law of the Old Testament. So their status as compared to others would have been associated with their high level of education. We must not confuse them with the "high" priest who mirrored the role of Moses (Luke 19:47). We must also note that under Roman rule, the high priest position seems to take on more of a legal or political role rather than a spiritual one. This group had education and connections.

Also, if a leading priest ascended to fill a seat on the Sanhedrin, it was common for that person to pass on that seat to progeny. While a priest of one generation might have known the Scriptures, that was not always the case with the next generation. Prominent families held power, so lineage comes into view as a determining factor for service among the seventy. For an example of this, consider the scene of the arrest of Jesus in John 18:12–13, and note that the high priest role passed to a relative.

> [12] Then the detachment of soldiers with its commander and the Jewish officials arrested Jesus. They bound him [13] and brought him first to Annas, who was the father-in-law of Caiaphas, the high priest that year.

The Pharisees surface as the other prominent group who actually dominated the seventy. They gained status through their knowledge of the Torah, the written law, coupled with the Halakha, the oral law (which represented a compilation of the oral traditions for interpreting the written law). Because they filled the majority of the seats in the Sanhedrin, their interpretation of biblical texts prevailed over the people. Literally, they ruled!

Famous Pharisees include Nicodemus and the apostle Paul. Attaining this level in the Jewish society gave Nicodemus the distinction of ranking as a "ruler" over the people (John 3:1), and also helped deliver the apostle Paul from a sticky situation (cf. Acts 23:1–11). Few people messed with leading Pharisees.

Rather than specifically identifying elders and officials of proven spiritual maturity and demonstrated administrative gifting like the Council of Moses, the members of the Sanhedrin appointed family members and/or friends with education and some measure of wealth to rule with them and help preserve power and tradition.

This shift reflects the cultural and political pattern for selecting overseers rather than choosing them according to the biblical paradigm. The Sanhedrin shifted to selecting rulers and leaders like the world does rather than locating overseers following the pattern set forth by the Lord. To avoid this snare, governing boards would do well to map a selection process that aligns with the biblical pattern.

2. Ruling and Controlling Posture

This second snare turns our attention to the change in the function of the Sanhedrin as compared to the Council of Moses. The Sanhedrin sat together, taking a posture of ruling and controlling rather than standing and listening to govern as humble servants. Acts 4:1–10 demonstrates this deleterious posture vividly.

> [1] The priests and the captain of the temple guard and the Sadducees came up to Peter and John while they were speaking to the people. [2] They were greatly disturbed because the apostles were teaching the people, proclaiming in Jesus the resurrection of the dead. [3] They seized Peter and

John and, because it was evening, they put them in jail until the next day. ⁴ But many who heard the message believed; so the number of men who believed grew to about five thousand.

⁵ The next day the rulers, the elders and the teachers of the law met in Jerusalem. ⁶ Annas the high priest was there, and so were Caiaphas, John, Alexander and others of the high priest's family. ⁷ They had Peter and John brought before them and began to question them: "By what power or what name did you do this?"

⁸ Then Peter, filled with the Holy Spirit, said to them: "Rulers and elders of the people! ⁹ If we are being called to account today for an act of kindness shown to a man who was lame and are being asked how he was healed, ¹⁰ then know this, you and all the people of Israel: It is by the name of Jesus Christ of Nazareth, whom you crucified but whom God raised from the dead, that this man stands before you healed."

Notice how the rulers and elders who orchestrated the crucifixion of Jesus are at work trying to maintain their control over the people. Their efforts backfired as the arrest of the apostles only serves to inspire others to believe the gospel of Jesus Christ. Despite their coordinated efforts, these formidable families and their co-conspirators fail to sustain their stronghold over the Jewish people.

There is a lesson here that holds true through human history. When a group tries to control and rule over work that belongs to God it is just a matter of time before things will unravel!

3. Idolatry to Money

The religious leaders kept their power over the people, in part, because they had access to financial resources associated with their interpretation of the law. Numerous examples illustrate this.

For example, when a Jewish man died, the widow had few rights, and biblical texts like Mark 12:38–40 (cf. Luke 20:47) reveal that her resources could be pillaged by those who ruled. Almost certainly, the religious leaders' excuse for this was that they did it for the good of the people and to preserve the ongoing work of their temple and their nation.

No wonder Jesus described the Pharisees as lovers of money in Luke 16:13–15! In antiquity, a lover of money was a person who thought that money made things happen.[7] In this setting where religion and rule had become one and the same, money emerged as the driving force, the power of the religious establishment.

> [13] "No one can serve two masters. Either you will hate the one and love the other, or you will be devoted to the one and despise the other. You cannot serve both God and money."
>
> [14] The Pharisees, who loved money, heard all this and were sneering at Jesus. [15] He said to them, "You are the ones who justify yourselves in the eyes of others, but God knows your hearts. What people value highly is detestable in God's sight."

This assessment of the religious leaders explains how and why they would allow merchants and money changers into the temple. Greedy for gain, they would benefit from the excessive revenue as various texts reveal (cf. Matthew 21:12–17; Mark 11:15–19; Luke 19:45–48; John 2:13–16).

The detestable nature of the religious leaders also elucidates why vices such as "lover of money" (1 Timothy 3:3) and "greedy for gain" (Titus 1:7) emerge as disqualifying factors for the office of overseer in the early church in the New Testament, because the "desire for money" or "greed," is idolatry (Ephesians 5:5; Colossians 3:5).

It is fitting that those who wrestle to gain control of God's work find that they need resources to rule. Consequently, they fall into the snare of idolatry to money to preserve their place of power in relationship to the people.

To avoid this snare, governing boards need to resist the tendency toward controlling and ruling. Additionally, overseers will benefit by implementing intentional stewardship and resource development measures so that each organization they serve maintains a right relationship to money.[8]

4. Pride

The Sanhedrin arrogantly aimed at preserving the status quo and its position between the Jewish people and in the Roman authorities. Remember the Sanhedrin's efforts to arrest and kill Jesus aimed at keeping peace with Rome and safeguarding, in its words, "both our temple and our nation" (John 11:48).

These leaders spoke with pride as if it was their house rather than God's house. Furthermore, to preserve their grip over their people they had the smug audacity to bring forward bogus testimonies when no fault could be found in Jesus as Matthew 26:57–59 shows.

> [57] Those who had arrested Jesus took him to Caiaphas the high priest, where the teachers of the law and the elders had

assembled. [58] But Peter followed him at a distance, right up to the courtyard of the high priest. He entered and sat down with the guards to see the outcome. [59] The chief priests and the whole Sanhedrin were looking for false evidence against Jesus so that they could put him to death.

When a governing group desires to maintain the status quo and uphold traditions at all costs, it leads them to commit horrible atrocities. Overseers that succumb to the snare of pride do the unimaginable. It happened back then and still takes place today. When any church or nonprofit board, motivated by excessive self-confidence, talks or acts as if they rule, they are guilty of the sin of pride. The only right course is repentance, which means to change directions.

For a biblical example of corporate repentance coupled with community reform, governing boards may choose to study texts like Ezra 7–10. Corporate repentance and community reform that start at the top can help churches and ministries collectively rediscover their role and fulfill their responsibilities.

Summary

Whereas the Council of Moses stood with God's servant, reflecting a readiness to listen to God and share the burden of the people, the Jewish Council of the first century, the Sanhedrin, appears in the opposite posture. Priests and Pharisees along with elders sat together as rulers and focused on doing whatever was necessary to preserve their position of power and traditions. Their efforts aimed at controlling the behavior of the people they supposedly served. While the size of the council had remained the same into the first century, the function and composition had shifted dramatically. The religious leaders lost sight of their responsibility to govern under God's rule and heaped burdens on the people as lovers of money. Larger cultural factors in the Roman world likely contributed to this seismic shift.

Chapter Three

The Gentile Councils of the Roman World

"Rome deliberately and systematically subverted the Greek ideal of the boulē ["council"] as the executive committee of an ekklēsia ["assembly"] whose membership changed regularly and often. Such potential instability was deemed intolerable. Rome was too clever to modify the traditional institutions of the Greek cities, because that would have been deeply resented. Instead it preserved the form while radically changing the content. It introduced a property qualification for membership in the ekklēsia and tended to grant its members life tenure. Thus, Rome ensured that whatever power the city retained was wielded by those with an aversion to change and a strong personal interest in preserving the status quo."[9]
Jerome Murphy-O'Connor

A "council" of trusted local officials governed communities under Greek rule in the Mediterranean world for centuries leading up to the days of the early church in the first century. This "council" was a subset of a larger group, known as the "assembly," which commissioned the council with authority to govern behavior within each city under the gaze of the pantheon of gods. Consequently, the common people honored the oversight of local councils and respected traditions associated with local deities.

When the center of power shifted from Greece to Rome after the Battle of Corinth (146 B.C.), Rome carefully kept the form of the local council but markedly changed how it functioned as explained above by Jerome Murphy-O'Connor. In introducing property ownership as a requirement for council membership, rich families would become ensconced in power for generations. Rome did this to maintain the state of affairs in perpetuity. It worked, at least for nearly 200 years. This time frame became widely known as *Pax Romana*, "Roman Peace" (27 B.C. – A.D. 180), though the term represents a misnomer at best because the common person experienced little peace in this era.

Priests also played a key part in local rule. Like their wealthy council counterparts, they passed on their positions to their offspring. Rome wanted it this way and identified key cities such as Ephesus, the Roman capital of Asia Minor, in which to locate imperial temples with cultic officials.

Acts 19:23–41 – The Cultural Factors in the First Century

"There was one citizen of Ephesus who was particularly alarmed
by the peoples' riotous conduct. This was the town clerk,
the executive officer of the civic assembly,
who took part in drafting the decrees to be laid out before it,
and had them engraved when they were passed.
He acted also as liaison officer between the civic government
and the Roman provincial administration,
which had its headquarters in Ephesus."[10]
F.F. Bruce

We learn about the councils of the Roman world in literary and inscription evidence from prominent cities like Rome, Athens, and Ephesus. The epigraphic data specifically presents a wide array of edicts made by "the council and the assembly" in these cities. Those words regularly appear at the beginning of official council proclamations to the people. We can read them on the stones in which they were etched and set in public places. Many exist to this day.

We also have biblical record of the proceedings of one such assembly in Ephesus recorded by Luke in Acts 19:23–41. This text that features the Council of Ephesus brings to light cultural factors in the first century related to the topic of governance.

> [23] About that time there arose a great disturbance about the Way. [24] A silversmith named Demetrius, who made silver shrines of Artemis, brought in a lot of business for the craftsmen there. [25] He called them together, along with the workers in related trades, and said: "You know, my friends, that we receive a good income from this business. [26] And you see and hear how this fellow Paul has convinced and led astray large numbers of people here in Ephesus and in practically the whole province of Asia. He says that gods made by human hands are no gods at all. [27] There is danger not only that our trade will lose its good name, but also that the temple of the great goddess Artemis will be discredited; and the goddess herself, who is worshiped throughout the province of Asia and the world, will be robbed of her divine majesty."
>
> [28] When they heard this, they were furious and began shouting: "Great is Artemis of the Ephesians!" [29] Soon the whole city was in an uproar. The people seized Gaius and Aristarchus, Paul's traveling companions from Macedonia,

and all of them rushed into the theater together. [30] Paul wanted to appear before the crowd, but the disciples would not let him. [31] Even some of the officials of the province, friends of Paul, sent him a message begging him not to venture into the theater.

[32] The assembly was in confusion: Some were shouting one thing, some another. Most of the people did not even know why they were there. [33] The Jews in the crowd pushed Alexander to the front, and they shouted instructions to him. He motioned for silence in order to make a defense before the people. [34] But when they realized he was a Jew, they all shouted in unison for about two hours: "Great is Artemis of the Ephesians!"

[35] The city clerk quieted the crowd and said: "Fellow Ephesians, doesn't all the world know that the city of Ephesus is the guardian of the temple of the great Artemis and of her image, which fell from heaven? [36] Therefore, since these facts are undeniable, you ought to calm down and not do anything rash. [37] You have brought these men here, though they have neither robbed temples nor blasphemed our goddess. [38] If, then, Demetrius and his fellow craftsmen have a grievance against anybody, the courts are open and there are proconsuls. They can press charges. [39] If there is anything further you want to bring up, it must be settled in a legal assembly. [40] As it is, we are in danger of being charged with rioting because of what happened today. In that case we would not be able to account for this commotion, since there is no reason for it." [41] After he had said this, he dismissed the assembly.

Here, the city clerk brought calm to a riot with a brief statement affirming the renown of the goddess and reminding everyone that

Rome gave them courts for solving disputes. He was motivated to call for order, because if the city was charged with rioting, Rome might take forceful measures to restore peace. No city wanted Rome to send soldiers to bring peace by force.

Gentile councils of the Roman world in the first century contained wealthy citizens and priests who were highly motivated to preserve the status quo. This explains why one affluent family dynasty, "the Herods," would rule Judea as a client state of Rome in the days of the birth, ministry, death, and resurrection of Jesus Christ (cf. Matthew 2, *et al*).

Cultural and political factors dictated by Rome shaped the governance structures across the Mediterranean world in the first century, impacting both Gentiles and Jews. Local councils like the one in Ephesus had little choice but to follow the Roman patterns for appointing officials, settling disputes, and controlling behavior in the cities. Those who failed to fulfill their duties faced either replacement or the threat of violence.

Four Pitfalls of Gentile Councils

As a result of the dominant cultural factors, four pitfalls come into view from the Gentile councils of the first century related to governance. Scripture sets them forth for our benefit. Spelling them out helps overseers learn how not to govern.

1. Selecting People of Status

The Ephesians listened to the city clerk because they voted that person into the position for a term of service from a ballot of land-owning citizens and because the city clerk was the liaison to

Rome. Culturally, the city clerk was an Ephesian, or one of them. They would have wanted it to stay that way.

The cultural, religious, and political patterns were interconnected and prescribed that candidates for community oversight had to be landowners. This requirement pointed to a significant level of wealth. These community officials must also exhibit the ability to keep the peace in order to retain the role. If they failed, an outsider sympathetic to Rome would replace them, which would create further tension.

For a biblical example of this, consider Marcus Antonius Felix. He was an influential courtier and freedman to Roman Emperor Claudius who ruled from A.D. 41–54. When Felix served as "governor" of Judea (Acts 23:24), Luke reports that Felix held the apostle Paul in custody as a favor to the Jews while hoping for a bribe (c. A.D. 56–58). When the apostle Paul offered no bribe, Felix was replaced by Porcius Festus (cf. Acts 24:26–27). The rules of the Roman governance game went something like this: pad your pockets by taking bribes and keep the peace by giving favors and resolving clashes in the community or get replaced.

Rome situated wealthy families in positions of oversight in Asia Minor, Judea, and across the ancient Mediterranean world by making property ownership a requirement for civic service. When that failed, the emperor sent prominent Romans to do the job. This shaped governance structures for both Gentiles and Jews. The cultural pattern prescribed appointments linked to wealth and relationships rather than the biblical paradigm that prioritizes the identification of candidates with proven spiritual maturity and demonstrated administrative gifting.

In contemporary practice, biblically-qualified candidates may also have some measure of wealth or status. To avoid the pitfall in view here, avoid catering to cultural pressures. Look for people of spiritual maturity and proven administrative gifting regardless of their measure of wealth or status. Some will have wealth and status, and some will not. The key is not to allow external traits fool you; look for people of internal depth!

2. Ruling and Controlling Posture

Notice again the governing control of the city clerk over the Ephesian council and assembly in Acts 19:35–41. In response to the riot, the city clerk initially appealed to the authority of the goddess, Artemis, whom they widely believed had power over the people. Basically, the city clerk directed them to calm down, believing that Artemis still reigned though idol sales had slid. Then the city clerk urged them to relax lest Rome send troops to restore order by force. That statement turned the tide of the meeting. No one wanted Rome to find out about the riot.

Gentile councils like this one in Ephesus knew their governance or rather, their rule, was directly linked to their connection to Rome. If that relationship eroded, not only would outside replacements ascend to rule, drastic measures would follow. For a tragic example of this, consider what took place in Jerusalem. Josephus, a famous Jewish historian, recounts that opposition to local oversight led to riots, so that by A.D. 66, troops were deployed (*The Wars of the Jews* 2.14.6). Eventually by A.D. 70, Rome trampled the city.

Rather than standing in service and listening to God like the Council of Moses, councils in the Roman world upheld the renown of local gods and maintained the status quo to retain rule. Those who governed sat as leaders ensconced in power with their ears set to Rome. They did as they were told. Those who failed to comply suffered harsh consequences. This explains why local authorities were so highly motivated to keep peace and preserve their place in society.

3. Idolatry to Money

The ministry of Paul in Ephesus (c. A.D. 52–54) contributed to the spreading of the gospel of Jesus Christ "so that all the Jews and Greeks who lived in the province of Asia heard the word of the Lord" (Acts 19:10). Though the renown of Ephesus had revolved around Artemis for centuries, the growing Christian movement was now taking market share. Idol sales fell. That's what really started the riot.

Demetrius and his fellow silversmiths stated plainly that they brought this case to the Council of Ephesus because their trade had deteriorated. The tipping point, however, was financial. The riot revealed that material wealth was a bigger idol for Ephesians than Artemis. The selling of pagan supernatural objects was big business. There was a lot of money tied up in it. Luke reports the value of such items in Acts 19:18–20.

> [18] Many of those who believed now came and openly confessed what they had done. [19] A number who had practiced sorcery brought their scrolls together and burned them publicly. When they calculated the value of the scrolls, the total came to fifty thousand drachmas. [20] In this way the word of the Lord spread widely and grew in power.

As a drachma represented about a day's wages, this was likely a huge blaze. This scene also reveals the explosive growth of the Christian community and may explain, at least in part, why idol sales had fallen so much. While the mob was determined to lynch the apostle Paul for sending them into financial crisis, the Council of Ephesus contributed to running him out of town for advancing the gospel of Jesus Christ rather than the renown of Artemis.

Either God or money serves as the power and driving force of the councils in the biblical record. For the Council of Ephesus, the desire for money surfaces as the guiding force of the proceedings and provides a sobering example for future governing groups.

Councils today face the same choice, whether to serve God or money. When a council shifts from governing to ruling, generally it will also shift from serving God to serving money, as money emerges as the only remaining power to fuel operations. Such councils often resort to secular fundraising practices aimed only at getting money from people rather than diligently engaging the participation of constituents and growing givers who are rich toward God.

4. Pride

The appeal of Demetrius along with his fellow silversmiths to the Council of Ephesus circles around preserving the reputation of the city and its regional prominence. He packages his remarks with specific language that reveals a desire to defend their local pride. The Ephesian masses respond by rioting.

We can almost hear their cries shouted for two hours as Luke reports twice (Acts 19:28, 34): "Great is Artemis of the Ephesians!" The goddess is not just "Artemis," but "Artemis of the Ephesians." Their chants dripped with pride. She was their local deity who had international acclaim, and they wanted it to stay that way!

Ancient sources tell us that her temple was both an architectural marvel and a tourist attraction that welcomed visitors from across the ancient world. For example, Antipater of Sidon named her temple one of the "Seven Wonders of the World," listing it second in prominence only to Mount Olympus (*Greek Anthology* 9.58). No wonder the city clerk acted to safeguard local pride and the reputation of the city in society!

Ultimately, the pride of the Council of Ephesus aimed at preserving the honor of Artemis, the prominence of their city, and their local authority in perpetuity. Councils face the same temptation in their service today. Be wary of any efforts that appear as self-promoting or that focus on expanding your own renown, rather than celebrating and rallying people to participate in efforts that extend God's name and fame.

Summary

Ancient sources report that Gentile councils in the first century like the Council of Ephesus appointed local members based on wealth and status. The council members retained those roles by preserving the status quo as dictated by Rome. We can trace how the desire to maintain control, idolatry to money, and pride guided governance proceedings. This analysis also helps us understand factors that likely influenced how the Jewish Council of the first century, the Sanhedrin, had drifted so far from the paradigm of the Council of Moses. It seems to have assimilated into Roman cultural trappings for the sake of self-preservation. As watchful observers, we must not overlook the instructive aim of the biblical record of the Council of Ephesus. It teaches us that worldly governance patterns and gospel efforts cannot go together.

Chapter Four

The Jerusalem Council in Acts of the Apostles

"It is no exaggeration to say that Acts 15
is the most crucial chapter in the whole book."[11]
Ben Witherington

Next, we consider the Jerusalem Council in Luke's Acts of the Apostles. The Jewish disciples of Jesus had just come to grips with the fact that Gentiles had also been granted "repentance that leads to life" (Acts 11:18). Consequently, a new sort of people had surfaced in the world. Their identity as followers of Jesus ran deeper than the ethnic labels, thus, "the disciples were called Christians first at Antioch" (Acts 11:26).

The defining traits of this new people, however, were quite unclear. For example, debate swirled around whether or not the Gentiles had to be circumcised like their fellow Jewish believers. This was not a small issue. The Jerusalem Council would sort it out and, in so doing, give us keen insights related to governance.

Acts 15 – The Governance of the Jerusalem Council

"In the council chamber citizens gathered to make decisions
about what actions should be taken in the future,
and how the city (or some of its constituents) should respond...
Acts 15 presents a series of speeches even more overtly
deliberative in nature,
as the Christian council chamber members debate whether or not
they will require Gentiles to be circumcised."[12]
David A. DeSilva

Some aspects of this pivotal council meeting for the early church appear more public. They transpire before the larger "church" or the "assembly," (*ekklēsia* in Acts 15:3, 4, 22, 41). While this wider group includes some from "the party of the Pharisees" (Acts 15:5), the council takes on a distinctly Christian composition when compared to other Jewish councils in the first century, containing only "apostles and elders" (Acts 15:6).

Our knowledge of the chamber proceedings is limited to the proverbial minutes provided by Luke, who records speeches or statements by Peter (Acts 15:7–11), Paul and Barnabas (Acts 15:12), and James (Acts 15:13–21) along with the letter to be circulated widely (Acts 15:22–29).

In the end, the Jerusalem Council makes a decision that shapes the future for all Christians, both Jewish and Gentile believers. Let's read the text in its entirety to see what biblical insights emerge pertaining to governance.

¹ Certain people came down from Judea to Antioch and were teaching the believers: "Unless you are circumcised,

according to the custom taught by Moses, you cannot be saved." ² This brought Paul and Barnabas into sharp dispute and debate with them. So Paul and Barnabas were appointed, along with some other believers, to go up to Jerusalem to see the apostles and elders about this question. ³ The church sent them on their way, and as they traveled through Phoenicia and Samaria, they told how the Gentiles had been converted. This news made all the believers very glad. ⁴ When they came to Jerusalem, they were welcomed by the church and the apostles and elders, to whom they reported everything God had done through them.

⁵ Then some of the believers who belonged to the party of the Pharisees stood up and said, "The Gentiles must be circumcised and required to keep the law of Moses."

⁶ The apostles and elders met to consider this question. ⁷ After much discussion, Peter got up and addressed them: "Brothers, you know that some time ago God made a choice among you that the Gentiles might hear from my lips the message of the gospel and believe. ⁸ God, who knows the heart, showed that he accepted them by giving the Holy Spirit to them, just as he did to us. ⁹ He did not discriminate between us and them, for he purified their hearts by faith. ¹⁰ Now then, why do you try to test God by putting on the necks of Gentiles a yoke that neither we nor our ancestors have been able to bear? ¹¹ No! We believe it is through the grace of our Lord Jesus that we are saved, just as they are."

¹² The whole assembly became silent as they listened to Barnabas and Paul telling about the signs and wonders God had done among the Gentiles through them. ¹³ When they finished, James spoke up. "Brothers," he said, "listen to me.

[14] Simon has described to us how God first intervened to choose a people for his name from the Gentiles. [15] The words of the prophets are in agreement with this, as it is written:

[16] "'After this I will return and rebuild David's fallen tent. Its ruins I will rebuild, and I will restore it, [17] that the rest of mankind may seek the Lord, even all the Gentiles who bear my name, says the Lord, who does these things'— [18] things known from long ago.

[19] "It is my judgment, therefore, that we should not make it difficult for the Gentiles who are turning to God. [20] Instead we should write to them, telling them to abstain from food polluted by idols, from sexual immorality, from the meat of strangled animals and from blood. [21] For the law of Moses has been preached in every city from the earliest times and is read in the synagogues on every Sabbath."

[22] Then the apostles and elders, with the whole church, decided to choose some of their own men and send them to Antioch with Paul and Barnabas. They chose Judas (called Barsabbas) and Silas, men who were leaders among the believers.[23] With them they sent the following letter:

The apostles and elders, your brothers, to the Gentile believers in Antioch, Syria and Cilicia: Greetings. [24] We have heard that some went out from us without our authorization and disturbed you, troubling your minds by what they said. [25] So we all agreed to choose some men and send them to you with our dear friends Barnabas and Paul— [26] men who have risked their lives for the name of our Lord Jesus Christ. [27] Therefore we are sending Judas and Silas to confirm by word of mouth what we are writing. [28] It seemed good to the Holy Spirit and to us not to burden you with anything beyond the following requirements: [29] You are to abstain from food sacrificed to idols, from blood, from the meat of strangled animals and from sexual immorality. You will do well to avoid these things. Farewell.

[30] So the men were sent off and went down to Antioch, where they gathered the church together and delivered the letter. [31] The people read it and were glad for its encouraging message. [32] Judas and Silas, who themselves were prophets, said much to encourage and strengthen the believers. [33] After spending some time there, they were sent off by the believers with the blessing of peace to return to those who had sent them. [[34]] [35] But Paul and Barnabas remained in Antioch, where they and many others taught and preached the word of the Lord.

[36] Some time later Paul said to Barnabas, "Let us go back and visit the believers in all the towns where we preached the word of the Lord and see how they are doing." [37] Barnabas wanted to take John, also called Mark, with them, [38] but Paul did not think it wise to take him, because he had deserted them in Pamphylia and had not continued with them in the work. [39] They had such a sharp disagreement that they parted company. Barnabas took Mark and sailed for Cyprus, [40] but Paul chose Silas and left, commended by the believers to the grace of the Lord. [41] He went through Syria and Cilicia, strengthening the churches.

"Certain people" stirred up trouble (Acts 15:1). They supposedly welcomed the inclusion of Gentiles to the community of faith, but only with the requirement that the Gentiles be circumcised to be saved. That was not a small hurdle to add to the gospel.

Does this bring flashbacks to your mind? Perhaps you recall situations in your church or ministry setting in which "certain people" with a broad knowledge of the Scriptures used that knowledge to heap burdens on others rather than serve them.

Not surprisingly, Paul and Barnabas got the cold shoulder from the Pharisees, despite the warm welcome of the church. Remember, the Pharisees were experts not only in the written law but also in its customary oral interpretation, so as we would expect, they mentioned Moses twice in their argument for the circumcision of the Gentile believers (Acts 15:1, 5).

On the other side of the table, James, who chaired the proceedings, also cited Moses with respect (Acts 15:21). With three references to Moses in Acts 15, and particularly the reference by James, we can surmise that the Jerusalem Council had a high regard for Moses and may have resolved to govern along the lines of the Council of Moses in Numbers 11. They would have had access to Numbers in the church in Jerusalem.

Scholars note widely that when Luke reported that "the apostles and elders met to consider this question," it probably took a while (Acts 15:6). We don't know how long they deliberated in the council chamber. What we do know, based on Acts, is that the proceedings shifted on the statements of key participants.

For example, Peter testified that he personally witnessed that the Gentiles received the Holy Spirit, and then he reiterated the core message of the gospel. Then, though Luke did not report the testimony of Paul and Barnabas (Acts 15:12), we know they spoke before James, the head of the church in Jerusalem, gave the closing statements, which effectively opened the door for the Gentiles to join the community of faith without having to undergo circumcision.

Does this remind you of a turning point in a board meeting? You can picture it in your mind. The more influential people at the table wait to let others speak and then, at just the right moment, contribute the decisive remarks to the deliberations.

Note the source of the pivotal words of James. He quoted Amos 9:11–12 from the Septuagint (the Greek translation of the Old Testament abbreviated as "LXX" as it was the work of seventy translators). With this citation in the heart language of Gentiles, James astutely announced that they were right to see themselves as sharers in the bearing of the name of Christ.

Ever been in situations when people debated at length and defended varying views and then finally someone authoritatively offered a biblical perspective? Often the only thing overseers can do to prepare for such situations is to know God's Word deeply as well as their audiences' understanding of Scripture. Mature overseers of deep spiritual maturity do that.

The decision of the council was both wise and welcoming, and its gravity grew when delivered by a multi-ethnic set of couriers. While these two were brothers in Christ and prophets (Acts 15:32), they probably had very different ethnic backgrounds. They were handpicked for the job. Judas (called Barsabbas) would have likely been the Greek equivalent to a Hebrew name, Judah, son of Sabbas, and Silas commonly occurs as a Greek version of the Roman name, Silvanus. Effectively, we deduce that a Jew and a Gentile delivered this news to bless and empower all listeners.

Occasionally, overseers are neither seen nor heard. They make decisions in closed chambers far away from the people they serve. The distance between the groups grows with limited communication, so the decisions come across like edicts from rulers. Alternatively, when overseers are both seen and heard or represented by couriers who embody their decisions, their governance can encourage and even unify a divided audience.

To save the best for last in the text, the Holy Spirit appears as the main character guiding the proceedings. This official statement reveals that the Spirit guided the council to this conclusion.

> "It seemed good to the Holy Spirit and to us not to burden you with anything beyond the following requirements. You are to abstain from food sacrificed to idols, from blood, from the meat of strangled animals and from sexual immorality. You will do well to avoid these things. Farewell" (Acts 15:28–29).

Notice that the letter does not even mention circumcision! Why? The issue was not theological but relational. For salvation, people did not need to do anything more because Jesus Christ finished the work. However, to preserve the unity of the Spirit, all Christians would do well to avoid activities associated with paganism (Acts 15:29).

Might this be the most powerful message of the Jerusalem Council for overseers? When deliberating on difficult issues, too often, overseers take sides and draw lines in the proverbial sand, which often results in division.

What if instead, each time, overseers resolve to look at situations through the lens of Scripture and to make decisions with the discernment of Solomon as recounted in texts like 1 Kings 3:9. "So give your servant a discerning heart to govern your people and to distinguish between right and wrong. For who is able to govern this great people of yours?" To pray for a discerning heart and to resolve to govern under God's rule will not make the issues overseers face any easier, but it might lead them to make decisions that preserve the unity of the Spirit and position God's work to multiply. In so doing, overseers remove the dispute from center stage and put the gospel of Jesus Christ back in the spotlight.

Similarities between Numbers 11 and Acts 15

> *"Moses's longing in Numbers 11 for the day when the Spirit would be poured out on all of God's people was played fortissimo in the prophets as they announced the "new thing" that "God would do in the last days." It was this hope of Moses that Peter saw being fulfilled not only with the thousands of Jewish converts (including some priests) but [also] with the conversion of the Gentiles. Peter rebuffed the circumcision sect decisively at the Jerusalem Council, declaring God's fulfillment of His promise..."*[13]
> Michael Horton

Moses knew God intimately by communing with Him in the tent of meeting. Moses shouldered a big burden, helping a discontent nation to know and follow the Lord. The newly formed people of God were like wayward children who did not know any better than to argue. While the council of seventy surely assisted him in humble service, he undoubtedly longed for the day when all of God's people would have the Spirit poured out on them.

Likewise, Peter, the "rock" on which Jesus Christ promised to build His Church (Matthew 16:18), had seen the Spirit poured out on both Jews and Gentiles. He got a glimpse of the fledgling family of God as a multi-ethnic mosaic of people. The tide of the council turned when, after lengthy discussion, Peter stood up and spoke (Acts 15:6–7). He made sure the yoke that his Jewish ancestors could not bear would not burden anyone any longer.

Even a casual reader can draw comparisons between Numbers 11 and Acts 15. When God formed His people both as a Jewish nation in the Old Testament and as an international Christian community in the New Testament, we see a council of overseers with similar composition and commission. Both texts serve as pivotal governance passages in the larger narrative of God's interaction with His people. In them, we observe four significant similarities based on this study of both passages.

1. Spiritual Maturity and Administrative Gifting

In Numbers 11:16, the overseers identified for service are described as "elders of the people and their officials" (NASB). They had tested character and trusted reputations. They were known to Moses, hand-picked administrators qualified to govern.

Correspondingly, Acts 15:6 reports a council with "apostles and elders," who had deep faith and spiritual maturity as pillars in the early church. They were known and respected because of their close relationship with the Lord Jesus Christ.

The presence of overseers with recognized spiritual maturity and demonstrated giftedness in Numbers 11 and Acts 15 appears in contrast to other councils in the biblical record. A closer look reveals that their composition differed because the selection processes followed very different aims.

The other councils appointed people from prominent families with wealth or status to governance roles. We also have record that they gave council seats to their offspring or friends. The councils in Numbers 11 and Acts 15 appear instead to follow God's design and desire for the selection and character of overseers. They are humble servants with proven spiritual maturity and demonstrated gifting.

2. Standing and Listening Posture

In Numbers 11 and Acts 15, the overseers appear in a posture that demonstrates respect and submission to the word of the Lord. For the Council of Moses, the overseers gathered and listened at the tent of meeting in order to serve. That was the place Moses heard God's voice. We can conclude that the elders and officials relied on wisdom from the Lord to stand with Moses and share the burden of governing the people.

This picture of standing and listening to God's Word differs manifestly from the Sanhedrin and the Council of Ephesus. The former considered governance as "sitting together" in seats passed on to progeny and people of status in order to rule based on oral law and tradition. The latter followed cultural patterns for the practice of oversight and served other deities rather than the God of the Scriptures.

Comparable to the Council of Moses who led "God's people" just after they had received that label, when Peter stood up in the Jerusalem Council which gathered shortly after followers of Jesus were first called "Christians," his remarks coupled with the comments of those who spoke after him, worked together to facilitate the exponential growth of the Christian movement. In both instances, the councils stood taller than any challenge. They stood taller—not because of some measure of human leadership or skill—but because they appear as overseers willing to govern in submission to God and His Word.

The Jerusalem Council knew the Scriptures, so it is fitting that the head of the church in Jerusalem, James, would consider the debate through the lens of Scripture. Specifically, he cited the Greek translation of the Old Testament, a text that the Gentile audience in question would likely have understood (Acts 15:16–17; Amos 9:11–12 in the LXX).

Remember, the image of standing and listening is about serving in submission and respect of God's rule. Though the biblical record presents the Sanhedrin and the Council of Ephesus as seeking to maintain their own rule, the Jerusalem Council focused on submitting to God's authority in alignment with His Word.

Also, the Jerusalem Council in Acts 15 gathered in the same place the Holy Spirit had been poured out on the day of Pentecost after the resurrection and ascension of Jesus Christ (Acts 2:1–13). The council and particularly the chair appear as listeners to each other and to God (Acts 15:19).

Unlike the other councils of the day, which are portrayed in the biblical record as talkers promoting their own agenda, these council members appear as divine listeners who hear the people and the word of the Lord for the people. They then govern based on what they have heard and discerned.

3. The Presence and Power of the Holy Spirit

The Holy Spirit showed up in a powerful way for Moses in the wilderness in Numbers 11. When the Lord poured out the Spirit on the seventy elders, they prophesied. This sign validated their divinely empowered appointment and confirmed their position.

Similarly, the Holy Spirit showed up as not merely in power in the proceedings in the Jerusalem Council, but as the guiding force. Their written proclamation demonstrates mystical deference to the Holy Spirit, "It seemed good to the Holy Spirit and to us…" and reveals to us that they aimed at following God's leading rather than leading themselves (Acts 15:28).

For both the Council of Moses and the Jerusalem Council, we witness the manifestation of the Spirit. The other councils in the biblical record have no such validation. This draws our attention to them as exemplary.

Discerning direction from the Lord takes time and requires margin for listening rather than talking in governance sessions. Gathering in silence to listen is not a new idea. We can trace it all the way back to the tent of meeting. Silence in board sessions might seem awkward to some, but it gives the Spirit space to speak to hearts that attune to God.

4. Humble Service

Back in Numbers 11, Moses was exasperated with the people of God. They brought all their problems to him. Their complaining was driving him crazy! The council of seventy helped by hearing disputes to restore relationships. They got their proverbial hands dirty to preserve unity and community under God's rule. This was vitally important, as God's people would journey together in the same big caravan for years. They had to get along!

Predictably, the Jerusalem Council in Acts 15 did not shy away in the face of a tough situation in shaping the identity of people now known as "Christians." The members neither met at night in secret like the Sanhedrin to make their decision nor followed cultural patterns for solving disputes like the Council of Ephesus. While the larger assembly knew what was going on, the council exhibited transparency in helping the people move from a place of "sharp dispute and debate" to a place of unity. The council's decision positioned gospel efforts to multiply, though as the latter part of the text reveals, further disagreements arose (Acts 15:39). Of course, as long as people are involved, conflicts will arise that may require further council intervention!

The Jerusalem Council entered the proverbial eye of the hurricane to locate a solution. It would not impose a burden on the Gentiles, but would release them from a yoke of slavery. The decision set them free to flourish as Christians, but they must look different than their pagan neighbors.

This decision effectively released power and upended the status quo. The implications of the situation cannot be understated. The Jerusalem Council gave away the power once reserved for Jews to position the Church to explode. In the flow of the biblical narrative, the Jerusalem Church decreased so the Jewish and Gentile Church could increase across the world.

Unlike the other councils in the biblical record, which in pride aimed at preserving their ruling dominance, the councils in Numbers 11 and Acts 15 reveal the opposite objective. They aimed at maintaining unity and easing the burdens of the people of God, even if that meant making decisions that would give away their power. That's precisely what they discerned the Spirit leading them to do in service to God's people.

Summary

After in-depth examination of the Jerusalem Council, this chapter set forth four similarities between the Council of Moses in Numbers 11 and the Jerusalem Council in Acts 15. Both councils contain members with proven spiritual maturity and demonstrated gifting. They stand in service in submission to God's rule as divine listeners who are guided by the Spirit. They humbly serve as overseers who make decisions that preserve unity among God's people. Together they help us envision a mindset for thinking about board governance from a biblical perspective.

······························· Chapter Five

Mindset: A Biblical Framework for Board Governance

"Later synods have acted and spoken in the same conviction, that the Holy [Spirit] governed the assemblies of the Church. Cyprian in his time wrote, in the name of the Council over which he presided, A.D. 252, to Pope Cornelius: 'It seemed good to us, under the guidance of the Holy Spirit...'"[14]
Charles Joseph Hefele

From our examination of the councils in Scripture, a mindset for thinking about board governance has surfaced. We find its roots in the paradigm of the Council of Moses in Numbers 11 and the practices of the Jerusalem Council in Acts 15. Also, it appears in stark contrast to the function of the Sanhedrin and the Council of Ephesus. In short, the biblical material helps us discern both how to think about governance and how not to think about it.

The early church councils report similar submission to the Spirit as the Jerusalem Council. For example, as noted above, Cyprian, Bishop of Carthage, echoes Acts 15:28 in his letter to Pope

Cornelius. We find a similar message in correspondence from the Council at Arles (A.D. 314). These citations suggest that the early church councils aimed at following the example of the Jerusalem Council. That said, this mindset is not new. We are just articulating it afresh for present and future generations.

The Four Components of the Council Mindset

> *"James' proposal of Gentile Christian abstinence*
> *in four cultural areas seemed a wise policy*
> *to promote mutual tolerance and fellowship."*[15]
> John R.W. Stott

Like the four-part decision of the Jerusalem Council, we suggest four components come together to form this mindset. We set them forth here with four statements. Each one employs the term "abstain" following the example of James in the Jerusalem Council. Admittedly, "abstain" is a strong word. James used it to shine light on behaviors to sidestep at all costs (Acts 15:20). We repeat it because we want governing boards to escape the snares of the Sanhedrin and the pitfalls of the Council of Ephesus.

We also use the word "adopt," and more specifically, the present participle form, "adopting," in each of the four statements. This word suggests that boards, in an ongoing way, espouse the characteristics from the Council of Moses and the Jerusalem Council. Simply put, we believe overseers will do well to follow the exemplary biblical framework on governance in perpetuity.

Also, we express this mindset descriptively rather than prescriptively by setting forth four patterns to circumnavigate, coupled with four practices to target. While we include illustrations from Scripture for each, we do not prescribe how to implement this mindset as that may vary in different settings.

For practical "how-to" suggestions that are more concrete and down-to-earth in nature, we suggest you dig into other books that contain a wealth of wise ideas.[16] We pray this biblical mindset shapes your thinking about governance while other helpful resources guide your practice of governance.

1. Abstain from allowing wealth, status, and/or lineage to serve as guiding factors for selecting overseers by adopting a selection process that places a priority on Christian maturity and administrative gifting over other candidate criteria.

We are not saying to abstain from engaging people whom God has blessed with material wealth or high status. We simply advise that you look for candidates of godly character and demonstrated gifting regardless of their socio-economic status. Such people know God and know what it takes to administrate His work. They can provide invaluable counsel and oversight.

How did the early church select overseers? Most answer this question by pointing to the qualifications lists of 1 Timothy 3:1–7 or Titus 1:5–10. While these texts list character traits to look for in board candidates, we direct your attention to another text to stimulate your thinking about the selection process. Acts 1:21–26 reports how the eleven disciples filled the empty spot vacated by Judas. Remember, the eleven were not just any group of overseers. They governed the affairs of the early church!

> [21] Therefore it is necessary to choose one of the men who have been with us the whole time the Lord Jesus was living

among us, ²² beginning from John's baptism to the time when Jesus was taken up from us. For one of these must become a witness with us of his resurrection."

²³ So they nominated two men: Joseph called Barsabbas (also known as Justus) and Matthias. ²⁴ Then they prayed, "Lord, you know everyone's heart. Show us which of these two you have chosen ²⁵ to take over this apostolic ministry, which Judas left to go where he belongs." ²⁶ Then they cast lots, and the lot fell to Matthias; so he was added to the eleven apostles.

Notice the two layers of the selection process. One reflects the human role, and the other reveals God's part in guiding the process. For the eleven, they looked for a person known to them who had been with the Lord Jesus from the beginning. Two candidates met these criteria: Barsabbas and Matthias. For God's part, the eleven cast lots to allow God to show them who of the two would serve as the final member of the twelve.

Have you ever seen a board selection process that was unclear or appeared to be rigged? We are not talking about loaded dice or a coin with two heads, but rather a selection process that was vaguely outlined. As a result, it was ripe for abuse and exploitation! In contrast, think about this New Testament illustration regarding the selection of Matthias. Because the disciples cast lots, no one could say this process was manipulated.

In the ancient world of the Scriptures, in the days of both the Old and New Testaments, people broadly believed the gods had sway over the affairs of humankind. It was actually quite common to cast lots to interface with the gods or with the one true God. We find a memorable example of this related to God in Jonah 1:4–7.

⁴ Then the Lord sent a great wind on the sea, and such a violent storm arose that the ship threatened to break up. ⁵ All the sailors were afraid and each cried out to his own god. And they threw the cargo into the sea to lighten the ship.

But Jonah had gone below deck, where he lay down and fell into a deep sleep. ⁶ The captain went to him and said, "How can you sleep? Get up and call on your god! Maybe he will take notice of us so that we will not perish."

⁷ Then the sailors said to each other, "Come, let us cast lots to find out who is responsible for this calamity." They cast lots and the lot fell on Jonah.

Back in the case of the eleven in Acts 1, the lot fell on Matthias. We know little about Matthias, but Hippolytus of Rome provides one important clue (c. A.D. 235). In his work, *On the Twelve Apostles: Where Each of Them Preached, and Where He Met His End*, Hippolytus mentions "Matthias, who was one of the seventy." The seventy appear in Luke 10:1–12 as followers personally sent out on mission by the Lord Jesus. Who was Hippolytus? Ancient sources report that he was a disciple of Irenaeus, who was a disciple of Polycarp, who was a disciple of John, who numbered among the twelve. This ancient external testimony of Hippolytus corroborates the biblical evidence.

The selection process that identified Matthias in Acts 1 suggests that the eleven abstained from cultural patterns for choosing overseers based on wealth, status, and/or lineage. Instead, they adopted a process for locating at least two qualified candidates. Also, we see them employ an intentional practice to get their opinions out of the way so that God could make the final choice from among candidates that surfaced in the process.

Don't hear us prescriptively suggesting that every board casts lots to choose between candidates, though we know at least one board that follows this biblical example to allow the Holy Spirit to make the final choice. Hear us descriptively urging you to outline a process that hinders people from manipulating the outcome. Thus, we advise boards to structure the candidate identification processes carefully in order to locate prospects with Christian maturity and demonstrated gifting, and guard the selection process to avoid scheming and exploitation.

We must warn that governing bodies that include wealth as part of the selection criteria may reveal that "the love of money" has wormed its way into their oversight. "The love of money" is the bent that idolizes money. It leads people to think that money makes things happen, when in contrast, the Holy Spirit is the power of ministry. God's Word explicitly identifies "lovers of money" as disqualified from governing (1 Timothy 3:3).

Also, boards that look for candidates from prominent families known for elite educational backgrounds and worldly wisdom may borrow trouble in the process. Though your board may not have many of "noble birth" or high status as Paul describes the Christian community in 1 Corinthians 1:26–31, if you have Christ and overseers with spiritual maturity and administrative gifting, you have just what you need.

2. Abstain from the tendency to rule or control Christ-centered churches and organizations from a sitting posture by adopting a practice of standing and listening to the

reading of Scripture as a reminder, at every meeting, to govern under God's rule.

This standing and listening posture finds roots in the specific instructions to the Council of Moses. Additionally, we see it reflected in the Jerusalem Council, especially with regard to its use of the Scriptures. Please notice what happens when these factors come together. Overseers find their place in God's order where the One who rules is seated, and those who stand and listen are positioned to serve the One who is seated. Thus, we suggest standing and listening to God's Word as it teaches us His desires for us as His servants as we govern His work. In this light, governance comes into view as holding administrators accountable to perform faithful activities while helping them as needed as humble, willing servants.

Numerous biblical texts describe our Lord Jesus Christ as seated at the right hand of God the Father (cf. Matthew 26:64; Mark 14:62, 16:19; Luke 22:69; Acts 2:34; Ephesians 1:20; Colossians 3:1; and Hebrews 1:3, 8:1, 10:12, 12:2). These texts teach us that our Lord Jesus Christ rules with God the Father. Prior to His ascension to Heaven, Jesus promised to send the Holy Spirit, who came at Pentecost, and since then, serves as the power and guiding force of God's work, as we discover in John 14:16–17 and throughout Luke's Acts of the Apostles. Only God sits and rules. Contrary to cultural governance patterns, we never rule! We stand to administrate or to oversee God's work, as directed by God from His seated position.

Earlier in this study we mentioned the first part of Peter's speech to the "rulers and elders" of the Sanhedrin in Acts 4:1–10. Few biblical texts reveal that God's work cannot be ruled by human councils better than the verses that follow there, Acts 4:11–21.

[11] "Jesus is 'the stone you builders rejected, which has become the cornerstone.' [12] Salvation is found in no one else, for there is no other name under heaven given to mankind by which we must be saved."

[13] When they saw the courage of Peter and John and realized that they were unschooled, ordinary men, they were astonished and they took note that these men had been with Jesus. [14] But since they could see the man who had been healed standing there with them, there was nothing they could say. [15] So they ordered them to withdraw from the Sanhedrin and then conferred together. [16] "What are we going to do with these men?" they asked. "Everyone living in Jerusalem knows they have performed a notable sign, and we cannot deny it. [17] But to stop this thing from spreading any further among the people, we must warn them to speak no longer to anyone in this name."

[18] Then they called them in again and commanded them not to speak or teach at all in the name of Jesus. [19] But Peter and John replied, "Which is right in God's eyes: to listen to you, or to him? You be the judges! [20] As for us, we cannot help speaking about what we have seen and heard."

[21] After further threats they let them go. They could not decide how to punish them, because all the people were praising God for what had happened.

Human overseers cannot rule over the work of God, and they must never try! That was the unsuccessful aim of the Sanhedrin and the Council of Ephesus in the first century. To help governing boards avoid the slippery slope of ruling, we advise they take time to stand

and listen to the Word, though we will not prescribe how or when to do this in governance settings.

What activities should fill a board agenda? While other studies answer this question from a technical perspective more extensively, we suggest that overseers of Christ-centered churches and ministries prioritize time for standing and listening to the reading of Scripture. Allot margin for times of silence as well, to attune to the still, small voice of the Holy Spirit.

These spiritual practices, of course, must be coupled with standard board agenda components such as approval of minutes, matters for discussion or decision, administrative reports, and other items. This may sound impossible for boards that meet infrequently or have full agendas; however, many overseers have reported to us that including time for Scripture and silence guides them through their remaining duties.

To know more about the listening aspect of this second component of the council mindset, we do well to look at the epistle written by the chairperson of the Jerusalem Council himself, James. He was known as "James the Just" or "the half-brother of Jesus," and led both the Jerusalem Council and the Jerusalem Church. Consider his counsel to us in James 1:19–25.

[19] My dear brothers and sisters, take note of this: Everyone should be quick to listen, slow to speak and slow to become angry, [20] because human anger does not produce the righteousness that God desires. [21] Therefore, get rid of all moral filth and the evil that is so prevalent and humbly accept the word planted in you, which can save you.

²² Do not merely listen to the word, and so deceive yourselves. Do what it says. ²³ Anyone who listens to the word but does not do what it says is like someone who looks at his face in a mirror ²⁴ and, after looking at himself, goes away and immediately forgets what he looks like. ²⁵ But whoever looks intently into the perfect law that gives freedom, and continues in it—not forgetting what they have heard, but doing it—they will be blessed in what they do.

In his own words, James reminds us to be quick to listen to one another and slow to speak. We must also hear God's Word and be sure to do what it says. Notice that he exhorts us to do this repeatedly as we can be forgetful.

When we align our governance mindset and practices with the exemplary councils in the biblical record, and apply what we hear over and over, we find freedom and blessing. When we follow the advice of a prominent chairperson in Scripture, our oversight strengthens even more.

How can boards avoid the trap of ruling and controlling? Boards would do well to form a checklist. Outline legal responsibilities to the government as well as reports that administrators must compile for accreditors, denominational offices, or other related groups. Also, boards must assess their governance regularly, perhaps with a combination of self-assessment processes and the aid of outside counsel. Staff assessment looks at ways to hold administrators accountable for faithful activities they can report, and not outcomes or results that are out of human control.

We advise evaluation in five areas to ensure oversight avoids "the common path" on which boards tend to rule and control and stays on "the kingdom path" to help boards govern faithfully.[17] This chart illustrates the two paths.[18]

The Common Path	The Kingdom Path
Production-Driven Leadership	Steward Leadership
Expansion-Focused Strategies	Faithfulness-Focused Strategies
Earthly Oriented Metrics	Eternity-Oriented Metrics
Results-Based Management	Relationship-Based Management
Utilitarian View of Resources	Stewardship View of Resources

Boards that look for production-driven leaders, adopt expansion-focused strategies, measure success based on earthly oriented metrics, and manage people based on results with a utilitarian view of resources tend toward ruling and controlling rather than governing. Sadly, they also find themselves slaves to money, as that emerges as the one power they discover they need to grow their earthly empire.

Alternatively, boards that value steward leadership, employ faithfulness-focused strategies, use eternity-oriented metrics to measure success, and take a relationship-based management approach with a stewardship view of resources tend toward governing God's work faithfully. In so doing, their oversight contributes to the building of God's eternal kingdom.

From our study, we believe that the time a governing board spends standing and listening may represent the most productive part of their proceedings, as it also helps the overseers collectively preserve the unity of the Spirit.

Adopt the pattern of standing and listening to avoid the temptation of ruling and controlling, follow your checklist, and assess your oversight either internally or with external assistance. This will help your board focus on governing for God while staying on the kingdom path.

3. Abstain from idolatry to money by adopting standards of responsible stewardship to make sure that the Christ-centered churches and organizations you serve depend on the Holy Spirit rather than money as the power of ministry.

This third component of the biblical mindset calls for abstinence from the idolatry to money that overtakes councils who try to rule rather than govern, such as the Sanhedrin or the Council of Ephesus. In plain terms, once those two councils sat and ruled, they needed money to make things happen. Rather than recount again how those councils exhibited the sin of idolatry to money, we will explain how governing boards can remain free of it because we "cannot serve both God and money" (Matthew 6:24; Luke 16:13).

From a biblical perspective, the key to ministry sustainability is not stockpiling money, although that's what worldly advisors suggest. Ministry is sustained by putting money to work obediently and faithfully on the kingdom path. That's the paradox of administration and governance in God's abundant economy. What we hold back enslaves us in fear, and what we put to work faithfully tends to produce more than we had before (cf. Matthew 25:14–30).

We notice this pattern from the beginning of the establishment of the early church. The Holy Spirit arrived with power at Pentecost (Acts 2:1–13), Peter preached a sermon, three thousand souls came to faith (Acts 2:14–41), and they responded by handling money following the radical teachings of Jesus delivered to them by the apostles, and the growth continued as a byproduct of faithfulness as Acts 2:42–47 illustrates.

> [42] They devoted themselves to the apostles' teaching and to fellowship, to the breaking of bread and to prayer. [43] Everyone was filled with awe at the many wonders and signs performed by the apostles. [44] All the believers were together and had everything in common. [45] They sold property and possessions to give to anyone who had need. [46] Every day they continued to meet together in the temple courts. They broke bread in their homes and ate together with glad and sincere hearts, [47] praising God and enjoying the favor of all the people. And the Lord added to their number daily those who were being saved.

Elaborate money-fueled schemes did not make ministry happen; the Holy Spirit did. God sustained and grew the church through the obedience of the people to the instructions of Jesus as taught by the apostles. Despite fierce persecution from the Jewish ruling council, the church blossomed.

Texts such as Acts 4:32–37 and 6:1–7 associate early church expansion with the work of the Spirit coupled with faithful administration and attentive governance. Few texts, however, illustrate that money is not the power behind ministry better than Acts 8:18–24. In this scene, Peter, an overseer of the Christian movement, rebukes Simon, the wealthy new believer and former sorcerer, for thinking money could purchase the power of ministry.

> [18] When Simon saw that the Spirit was given at the laying on of the apostles' hands, he offered them money [19] and said, "Give me also this ability so that everyone on whom I lay my hands may receive the Holy Spirit."

[20] Peter answered: "May your money perish with you, because you thought you could buy the gift of God with money! [21] You have no part or share in this ministry, because your heart is not right before God. [22] Repent of this wickedness and pray to the Lord in the hope that he may forgive you for having such a thought in your heart. [23] For I see that you are full of bitterness and captive to sin."

[24] Then Simon answered, "Pray to the Lord for me so that nothing you have said may happen to me."

Simon had money and thought it could buy power. In the ancient world, many held this view. Sadly, this thinking prevails today in the secular world and sometimes among professing believers in Jesus Christ. Money does have power, so people with money who come to faith naturally think it can make ministry happen. Many boards demonstrate this belief.

When Simon saw the Holy Spirit, he witnessed a power greater than anything he had ever seen. As a new believer, it makes sense that he would think that money could purchase this power, but it showed he was captive to the sin of the love of money. Thus, Peter rebuked him and called him to repentance. This reflects a similar pattern to how Jesus set Peter straight, rebuking him for seeing things from a human point of view rather than from God's perspective (cf. Matthew 16:23).

Perhaps you can recall a board member who held the human view that money was the power for ministry? Whether or not someone such as the board chair graciously rebuked that person, we must announce the danger of allowing this thinking to exist on boards. It puts everything at risk! It can cause churches and organizations to drift away from participation with God in His work to merely doing good works with human power and financial resources. Such people have a tragic surprise when they someday meet the Lord (cf. Matthew 7:21–23).

Since all money belongs to God and comes from God, faithful administrators put God's money to work to accomplish His purposes. They do this with appropriate financial controls, and attentive overseers hold them accountable with tools such as budgets, reports, and audits.

How much cash should a church or ministry have on hand? Though this represents a technical question, we will answer it as it comes up often and because we feel we can offer a biblically-rooted answer. We broadly recommend three-months of income as a good target for the "money bag" (*glōssokomon* in John 13:29) or "common" fund (*koinon* in Acts 2:44; 4:32) because a *mina* (three-months of income) represented the measure Jesus used in a parable to suggest the sufficient level of financial resources for a steward to serve fruitfully (Luke 19:11–27).

Rather than prescribe that every church or ministry operate with three-months cash, we descriptively advise your board to work with your administrators to set a target. Think of this counsel as holding overseers and administrators accountable not to stockpile money for security. Functioning with a float such as three-months cash enables the ministry to have a "common" fund to cover operating expenses and remain in a place of perpetual dependence on God.

To sidestep disaster in an ongoing way, we suggest that every Christ-centered church and organization follow biblically-based standards to ensure the faithful administration of God's work. In the United States, we suggest adopting "ECFA's Seven Standards of Responsible Stewardship"™ that relate to doctrinal issues, governance, financial oversight, use of resources and compliance with laws, transparency, compensation-setting and related-party transactions, and stewardship of charitable gifts.[19]

Around the world, overseers, pastors, ministry administrators, lawyers, and accountants have adopted similar standards for the faithful governance and administration of Christ-centered churches and ministries.[20] Such standards help overseers work collaboratively with church or ministry staff to ensure the faithful oversight of God's work.

4. Abstain from pride by adopting rhythms of prayer and fasting before God, humble service toward others, and submission to peer accountability to verify compliance with standards of responsible stewardship.

The fourth and final component of the biblical mindset for governance calls overseers to abstain from the human proclivity to pride by adopting rhythms that put the board in a posture of humility before God, others, and their peers who do God's work with them. Ultimately, this point aims at preserving God's honor, because if pride brings down the board of a Christ-centered church or ministry, God's reputation gets tarnished in a widespread way before a watching world.

Jesus modeled prayer and fasting for us prior to His earthly ministry (cf. Matthew 4:1–11; Luke 4:1–13). He also gave explicit instructions on prayer and fasting in the heart of the Sermon on the Mount (cf. Matthew 6:5–18). It is fitting then that in Antioch, where followers of Christ were first labeled "Christians" (Acts 11:26), that the prophets and teachers ministering there engaged in prayer and fasting, which resulted in the launch of expansion of Christian mission. Acts 13:1–3 reflects this.

> [1] Now in the church at Antioch there were prophets and teachers: Barnabas, Simeon called Niger, Lucius of Cyrene, Manaen (who had been brought up with Herod the tetrarch) and Saul. [2] While they were worshiping the Lord and fasting, the Holy Spirit said, "Set apart for me Barnabas and Saul for the work to which I have called them." [3] So after they had fasted and prayed, they placed their hands on them and sent them off.

Similarly, Paul and Barnabas appointed overseers in Acts 14:23 with prayer and fasting. "Paul and Barnabas appointed elders for them in each church and, with prayer and fasting, committed them to the Lord, in whom they had put their trust."

Prayer positioned them and positions us to receive God's guidance on the process, and fasting helps God's servants set aside their own desires or agendas on the decision or issue. The biblical record presents prayer and fasting as primary practices of overseers who seek after the heart of God.

Overseers also take a humble posture of service in relationship to others. They do this because it marks the way the Lord Jesus instructed the twelve to serve in Luke 22:25–27. This same twelve would become the overseers of the early church.

> [25] Jesus said to them, "The kings of the Gentiles lord it over them; and those who exercise authority over them call themselves Benefactors. [26] But you are not to be like that. Instead, the greatest among you should be like the youngest, and the one who rules like the one who serves. [27] For who is

greater, the one who is at the table or the one who serves? Is it not the one who is at the table? But I am among you as one who serves."

Overseers must avoid following the worldly pattern of ruling or lording over people. Instead, they must serve those entrusted to their care following the instructions and example of Jesus.

We also hear this counsel from the twelve themselves. For example, Peter echoes this sentiment by graphically saying "clothe yourselves with humility toward one another" (1 Peter 5:5). That's great advice from the one that Jesus appointed to serve as the proverbial chair of the Church (cf. Matthew 16:18)!

How can governing boards exhibit humble service? We advise them to look closely at the words and actions they communicate as a board. Specifically, scrutinize the perceptions that form in the minds of those served. Start by examining language. Remove all possessive talk like "our" church or "our" ministry. This helps root out pride from the human mind and heart.

For an illustration of this, see 1 Peter 5:1–3. Peter calls overseers to serve "God's" flock willingly, not for personal gain, but for the good of the group, as eager examples to "the" flock. Notice his careful avoidance of possessive language and emphasis on setting a good example.

[1] To the elders among you, I appeal as a fellow elder and a witness of Christ's sufferings who also will share in the glory to be revealed: [2] Be shepherds of God's flock that is under your care, watching over them—not because you must, but because you are willing, as God wants you to be; not

pursuing dishonest gain, but eager to serve; [3] not lording it over those entrusted to you, but being examples to the flock.

Likewise, Paul also testifies to service with humility following the leading of the Spirit. He sets forth that pattern explicitly in his remarks to the overseers of the church in Ephesus when he bids them farewell (c. A.D. 54) in Acts 20:17–22. Undoubtedly, he wants them to follow his example after his departure.

[17] From Miletus, Paul sent to Ephesus for the elders of the church. [18] When they arrived, he said to them: "You know how I lived the whole time I was with you, from the first day I came into the province of Asia. [19] I served the Lord with great humility and with tears and in the midst of severe testing by the plots of my Jewish opponents. [20] You know that I have not hesitated to preach anything that would be helpful to you but have taught you publicly and from house to house. [21] I have declared to both Jews and Greeks that they must turn to God in repentance and have faith in our Lord Jesus. [22] And now, compelled by the Spirit, I am going to Jerusalem, not knowing what will happen to me there."

The final aspect of this fourth component that comes into view to abstain from pride is peer accountability. Peer accountability celebrates the fact that all Christ-centered churches come together as God's Church, and all Christ-centered ministries work collectively doing God's work, so they would do well to hold each other accountable to follow standards of responsible stewardship in order to preserve God's honor and reputation.

Peer accountability takes shape in the USA when boards direct administrators to apply for accreditation with a group such as

ECFA. This action positions the organization to submit to a process that verifies compliance with the standards they profess to follow. Christ-centered churches and ministries in the USA that are found to meet "ECFA's Seven Standards of Responsible Stewardship"™ get to affix the ECFA seal on their materials.

Why affix a seal? ECFA and similar peer accountability groups in nations around the world affix a seal following the example of the apostle Paul. He employed a cultural practice of using a seal to enhance trust in the handling of charitable giving and to certify the integrity of the collection process. He reports using a seal in Romans 15:25–29 (NASB).

> [25] but now, I am going to Jerusalem serving the saints. [26] For Macedonia and Achaia have been pleased to make a contribution for the poor among the saints in Jerusalem. [27] Yes, they were pleased to do so, and they are indebted to them. For if the Gentiles have shared in their spiritual things, they are indebted to minister to them also in material things. [28] Therefore, when I have finished this, and have put my seal on this fruit of theirs, I will go on by way of you to Spain. [29] I know that when I come to you, I will come in the fullness of the blessing of Christ.

When Christ-centered churches and organizations humbly listen to outside counsel, engage in collaborative peer learning, voluntarily submit to peer accountability, and demonstrate compliance with standards by affixing a seal, it enhances trust and builds confidence for people to participate in God's work. This holds true globally, because these activities follow God's design for administration and governance.

More importantly, these actions protect Christ-centered churches and organizations from allowing pride to bring down what God has established in their midst by the power of the Holy Spirit. Remember, avoiding the pitfall of pride is about taking great pains to preserve God's honor and reputation.

Summary

Four statements come together to form a biblical mindset for board governance. We have presented them in a descriptive manner to help boards abstain from the snares of the Sanhedrin and the pitfalls of the Council of Ephesus. We suggest that boards will do well in adopting patterns that reflect the characteristics of the Council of Moses and the Jerusalem Council, as the Scriptures portray these councils as exemplary. We include the four components here again for your review.

1. Abstain from allowing wealth, status, and/or lineage to serve as guiding factors for selecting overseers by adopting a selection process that places a priority on Christian maturity and administrative gifting over other candidate criteria.

2. Abstain from the tendency to rule or control Christ-centered churches and organizations from a sitting posture by adopting a practice of standing and listening to the reading of Scripture as a reminder, at every meeting, to govern under God's rule.

3. Abstain from idolatry to money by adopting standards of responsible stewardship to make sure that the Christ-centered churches and organizations you serve depend on the Holy Spirit rather than money as the power of ministry.

4. Abstain from pride by adopting rhythms of prayer and fasting before God, humble service toward others, and submission to peer accountability to verify compliance with standards of responsible stewardship.

Chapter Six

Model: Spiritual Practices for Maintaining a Biblical Mindset

*"The apostles evinced their conviction
that the Holy Spirit is present in general councils,
when they published their decrees with this formula,
Visum est Spiritui sancto et nobis (it seemed good to the Holy [Spirit]
and to us), at the [Council] held at Jerusalem."*[21]
Charles Joseph Hefele

The councils after the Jerusalem Council identified a specific "formula" (or we prefer the word "model") to keep the Holy Spirit in charge. This formula or model demonstrated the desire to follow the example of the Jerusalem Council in the Scriptures: "It seemed good to the Holy Spirit and to us" (Acts 15:28).

Based on our biblical and historical research coupled with the discussion of the components of this mindset with various overseers, we believe that such a framework or model is necessary to help boards apply this biblical mindset. This model must be understood as simple but not simplistic. Any governing body can use it, but it will not necessarily make the hard work of governance any easier. It will, however, help overseers maintain the biblical mindset.

We believe that no governing board of a Christ-centered church or ministry wants to become a case study of disaster. No such council wants the story of their oversight to report how they morphed from governing like the Council of Moses to ruling and controlling like the Sanhedrin to maintain its place in society. The truth is, it could happen to any board. Similarly, no board wants to shift from governing like the Jerusalem Council to allowing greed to guide decisions like the Council of Ephesus. Again, it could happen to any board.

Consider this model as a set of guardrails to help your governing board stay on track in maintaining the biblical mindset. Think of it as a framework or model to keep the Holy Spirit in charge.

The Four Disciplines of the Council Model

> *"Daily prayer engages us in praying the psalms, prayerful reflection on a reading from Scripture, silent contemplation, and prayers of thanksgiving, intercession, and supplication. From ancient times, it has been a discipline that has enriched the life of faith. In maintaining this discipline, we are enriched knowing we are joined with others in prayer, our spiritual lives are deepened, and we are strengthened to persevere in the faith in the face of the invasive secularism that surrounds us."*[22]
> Harold M. Daniels

This section aims at setting forth a model with four disciplines that we would prefer to describe as formational rather than formulaic. Think of these four practices as descriptive rhythms that can transform overseers, rather than prescriptive behaviors that deliver results. When applied, we have found this model helps overseers maintain a biblical mindset for governance.

The council model includes four disciplines or practices: *Scripture, Silence, Sharing,* and *Supplication.* We suggest that boards block out specific time for the four practices at each meeting or at a set time each year when the board gathers for a longer meeting, such as a retreat. We recommend you start with the texts from the biblical record that recount the four councils in four separate sessions: Numbers 11; John 11:47–50; Acts 19:23–41; and Acts 15. From there, boards would do well to choose biblical texts that relate to topics they want to discuss at future meetings.

Whether in regular board sessions or in longer retreat settings, this model helps councils of Christ-centered churches and nonprofits attune to God as a group. Each of these four disciplines positions overseers and boards to govern spiritually in an increasingly secular society.

1. Scripture

Board members with whom we discussed this model reported the practice of having a devotional at the start of each meeting. We heard that response widely.

We suggest that such a devotional reading should represent the bare minimum use of Scripture for the board of a Christ-centered church or ministry. We say this because, in a Scripture-devoid meeting atmosphere, overseers might shift their thinking from "the Bible" to "the business at hand," and in so doing, shift from governing to ruling, and invite the danger of forgetting altogether that they govern God's work.

Some boards find richness in reading from Psalms at various junctures in the meeting. The way the Gospels portray Jesus illustrates that He likely prayed the Psalms (cf. Mark 14:26 and Psalms 113–118; Mark 15:34 and Psalm 22:1; Luke 23:46 and Psalm 31:5). Governing boards would do well to pray them too, so that the deep relationship with God the Father that we see in Jesus and that we see in David, Moses, and the other writers of Psalms, grows in our hearts as overseers. At longer retreats, some may choose to pray the Psalms at the divine hours.[23]

For constructive topics like board development, again, perhaps start with texts like Numbers 11; John 11:47–50; Acts 19:23–41; and Acts 15, and move to other biblical passages we have mentioned in this book, such as Ezra 7–10. If the board of a Christ-centered church or ministry comes to a meeting facing an issue or challenge, we advise standing and listening to what the Bible says on the topic. We offer this counsel because the Scriptures teach us how to think, how not to think, how not to live, and how to live as 2 Timothy 3:16–17 declares.

> [16] All Scripture is God-breathed and is useful for teaching, rebuking, correcting and training in righteousness, [17] so that the servant of God may be thoroughly equipped for every good work.

Overseers do well to grow in their knowledge of the Scriptures together. Stand and read them aloud to help your board govern with both "knowledge and understanding" (Jeremiah 3:15). The people stood when Ezra read God's Word, and Jesus followed this standing pattern too (cf. Nehemiah 8:5; Luke 4:16)

The Council of Moses stood and listened to the Lord at the tent of meeting to guide its governance service. In similar fashion, the Jerusalem Council found the key to resolving the sharp dispute came by hearing the Scriptures together.

2. Silence

Be still. This can be difficult for governing boards; however, when we shared this biblical model with overseers to test the ideas herein, many welcomed the practice of setting aside time for extended periods of silence. For some, it came across as a foreign practice that they felt might actually add value. Consider this explanation of the importance of silence by Richard Foster. Notice how it releases us from our human tendencies.

> Silence frees us from the need to control others. One reason we can hardly bear to remain silent is that it makes us feel so helpless. We are so accustomed to relying upon words to manage and control others. A frantic stream of words flows from us in an attempt to straighten others out. We want so desperately for them to agree with us, to see things our way. We evaluate people, judge people, condemn people. We devour people with our words. Silence is one of the deepest disciplines of the Spirit because it puts a stopper on that.[24]

Jesus modeled this discipline for us to hear from the Father (cf. Matthew 14:13; Mark 1:35). A few boards that we have worked with have taken time for silence to listen expectantly for the Spirit to speak. Those boards shared amazing stories of how God worked and guided the group.

Boards that have blocked out time to "be still" with silence have also testified that God guided strategic direction processes and, in so doing, transformed them into spiritual discernment experiences (Psalm 46:10). Silence helps bring people together in unity and also positions them to discern with clarity the direction God desires for them. Many boards combine silence with standing to attune to the Holy Spirit in a posture of submission.

Numerous boards that serve Christ-centered churches or nonprofits that have a physical location report doing prayer walks in silence to hear the Spirit speak regarding various facets of ministry. Silent retreats also come up in discussions as a practice for discerning direction from the Spirit. Another example might be for each board member to schedule an amount of time daily between board meetings to attune to the Spirit. Hear these ideas as descriptive examples of practical ways that overseers might position themselves to discern direction both collectively and individually.

We admit that these ideas presuppose that the overseers believe that God still speaks to hearts today if they attune to His voice. We believe the discipline of silence, whether during meetings or outside of governance sessions, helps overseers discern God's agenda rather than aiming at pushing some human set of plans.

3. Sharing

Particularly in the account of the Jerusalem Council, we see that each person on the governing body has a voice. No one overseer comes into view as more important than the others. That fits with how we might expect Christ-centered churches and ministries to operate, but many boards simply do not create space for open sharing based on the structure and flow of agendas. Often the board chair and committee chairs do most of the talking.

Boards that have tested this council model have reported that God provided clarity about complex topics that could have been contentious. He brought oneness regarding agenda items that could have taken a long time to discuss by knitting the board members' hearts together in the time spent reading Scripture and then through the silence and sharing. In other words, overseers indicated that they heard others saying what God seemed to be stirring in their own hearts. Because overseers aimed at listening to God and others, they said they actually spoke less, which created margin for everyone to share as they felt led (cf. James 1:19).

There are inevitably times when listening in silence may result in the perception of hearing "nothing" from God. Boards report that, at these times, the practice of combining committee discussions with open sharing helped them collectively to resolve to pray and wait on the Lord rather than feeling pressured to immediately discuss a solution. At these times, wait on the Lord together and perhaps read texts like Psalm 27 aloud.

As you wait on the Lord, include time for open sharing. Pour out your hearts to God as a governing body. This collective travail transforms the board and may contribute to an outpouring of the Holy Spirit as Billy Graham has noted.

> Before three thousand people were brought into the Church on the day of Pentecost, the disciples had spent fifty days in prayer, fasting, and spiritual travail...

This kind of prayer can span oceans, cross burning deserts, leap over mountains, and penetrate jungles to carry the healing, helping power of the gospel to the objects of our prayers.

This kind of mourning, this quality of concern, is produced by the presence of God's Spirit in our lives. That "the Spirit itself maketh intercession" indicates that it is actually God pleading, praying, and mourning through us. Thus we become co-laborers with God, actual partners with Him: Our lives are lifted from the low plane of selfishness to the high plane of creativeness with God.

John Knox travailed in prayer, and the Church in Scotland expanded into new life. John Wesley travailed in prayer, and the Methodist movement was born. Martin Luther travailed in prayer, and the Reformation was underway...

If we pray this kind of prayer, an era of peace may come to the world and hordes of wickedness may be turned back.[25]

Descriptively, think of sharing as giving everyone a voice so that the board can discern God's direction together. In too many cases, sharing in board settings appears as a few people pushing an agenda. Boards that block out time for sharing report that they learned insights from each other that they had not expected, which edified the larger group. In times when overseers feel that they hear nothing from God, they do well to direct their sharing heavenward in unison and with persistence (cf. Luke 18:1-8).

Again, human administration centers on inviting support for God's work and putting to work all that God supplies. From there, our supplication includes lifting up in prayer all we think we need from God with specific requests. Faithful overseers and administrators do not do this alone either; they rally constituents to join them in supplication.

The apostle Paul exhorts us along these lines in Philippians 4:6–7. Supplication or "prayer and petition with thanksgiving" guides boards away from worry to unimaginable peace. Through the practice of supplication, we position the board, staff, and all the constituents served by the organization whom we rally to pray with us to experience the incomprehensible peace of God.

> [6] Do not be anxious about anything, but in every situation, by prayer and petition, with thanksgiving, present your requests to God. [7] And the peace of God, which transcends all understanding, will guard your hearts and your minds in Christ Jesus.

Summary

We can trace that councils in the early church followed a formula to keep the Holy Spirit in charge. We suggest it includes at least four formational disciplines that, if applied, can help boards govern with a biblical mindset: *Scripture, Silence, Sharing,* and *Supplication.* Boards of Christ-centered churches and ministries that adopt these spiritual practices can, in so doing, discipline themselves to submit to the Holy Spirit and to govern like those exemplified in Scripture in an increasingly secular world.

4. Supplication

With this final aspect of the model, we suggest that boards tak
to lift up specific petitions to God, asking God to do what hu
cannot do. Perhaps throughout the board meeting, someon
take note of items that cannot happen without God's he
intervention. As Hudson Taylor noted, this represents the so
of power for ministry and mission.

> "Since the days of Pentecost, has the whole church ever pu
> aside every other work and waited upon Him for ten days
> that the Spirit's power might be manifested? We give too
> much attention to method and machinery and resources
> and too little to the source of power."[26]

For most governing boards, the only instances of prayer a
opening and closing meetings. That's hardly sufficient! Boar
cannot possibly oversee God's work without blocking extend
time for prayer, especially when one of the leading responsibilit
of the board is to ensure adequate resources for t
accomplishment of the mission. Remember, God, and not a
human agents, is the Supplier of those resources. So, go
governors hold administrators accountable to do the faithful wo
of inviting people to participate in God's work while calling on G
to supply. As the saying goes, they work as if it all depends on th
and pray because it all depends on God.

Also, boards would do well to adopt the perspective of Adonira
Judson when it comes to ensuring adequate resources for t
Christ-centered church or organization. "It is true that we m
desire much more. But let us use what we have, and God will g
us more."[27]

······· Chapter Seven

Map: Return to Arles and Ask Hard Questions

"Simply adopting a corporate model or modified corporate model of governance will not result in developing healthy Christian organizations... a new framework specifically developed for the Christian not-for-profit sector is required..."[28]
David Bartlett and Paul Campey

The council mindset gives overseers a new framework for thinking biblically about governance. The council model provides disciplines for maintaining this perspective at Christ-centered churches and ministries. But all this must be put to work! After reading this far into the book you may be asking, "Where should I go from here?" You want a map of sorts.

Because overseers and councils find themselves at different starting places, we prayed and reasoned at length regarding how to best point the way. To help your council govern according to the biblical perspective set forth in this book, we encourage you to do two things from here: return to Arles and ask hard questions (twenty of them). And, for those who want to dig deeper, take advantage of the study guide in the back of this book.

Return to Arles

"To the same effect the [Council] of Arles, A.D. 314,
expressed itself: "It seemed good, therefore,
in the presence of the Holy Spirit and His angels"
(Placuit ergo, præsente Spiritu Sancto et angelis ejus)."[29]
John Hardouin

There's an important reason we suggest you return to Arles, symbolically speaking, in order to find your way. But first, consider this background to put our exhortation in context.

We knew from the beginning of writing this book that Vincent van Gogh's *Café Terrace at Night,* painted in Arles, France (1888), would serve as the perfect cover image. Look closely into the café to see if you can discover why we chose it. Our Lord Jesus Christ appears to come into view as the central figure in the light of the café standing in service to the disciples and modeling the posture of service for future overseers like us.[30] We chose this painting as it illustrates the message of this book. What we did not know, however, was the mystical connection that the content of this book would have with Arles!

In the aforementioned research of Charles Joseph Hefele and John Hardouin on the councils of the early church, each council appears to have followed the same formula to govern under the rule of the Holy Spirit up to the Council at Arles in A.D. 314. After that, however, the tone of the evidence reveals that the councils under Constantine the Great and later appear to have shifted from governing to ruling. Not good!

So, in a sense, this book serves as a clarion call to overseers everywhere to return to Arles and adopt the perspective of that council, and the councils before it, tracing back to the Jerusalem Council of Acts 15 and the Council of Moses of Numbers 11. To return to Arles is to resolve to govern God's way by acknowledging the Holy Spirit, not ourselves, as the leader and guiding force of ministry. From there, we practice disciplines collectively, as outlined in this book, to "keep in step with the Spirit" (Galatians 5:16-26). Such rhythms help us make sure our boards govern in submission to God's rule. In perpetuity, we appear as humble, standing servants, following the example of our Lord Jesus Christ.

When you return to Arles, sit there a while. It took time for the ideas in this manuscript to take shape in our hearts, minds, and eventually on paper. It required research, testing, and numerous meetings. We gathered in café settings, on phone calls, and at conferences to discuss it. So when we look at *Café Terrace at Night*, we remember those meetings, and we acknowledge that this book ultimately came together only because our Lord Jesus Christ helped light the way for us.

Likewise, we pray the biblical perspective set forth in this book will enlighten your governance. So often in our governance, we can feel like we are lost or wandering in darkness, like the characters going different directions in the right side of the painting. Whenever you feel that way, walk toward the light. Take a seat with us in the café! We pray this book refreshes all who read it like a good cup of coffee or tea. In the *Café Terrace at Night*, we can learn together with the disciples who appear to surround our Lord Jesus Christ.

Perhaps put this painting on the wall of your office or boardroom to remind you to govern according to God's design. You can undoubtedly acquire a print for a minimal expense. But don't stop there! Ask hard questions of yourself and your council.

Ask Hard Questions

In submission to the Holy Spirit, we recommend that you use these twenty questions to help you and your fellow overseers align collectively as a council with the biblical perspective outlined herein. Go through them at one long board meeting or over many meetings. Put some effort into this process. You will only get out of it what you put into it.

On smaller boards, the board chair may choose to work through all the questions, or on larger councils, different questions may be assigned to various overseers. Either way, be sure to interface with other overseers and with ministry administrators to locate honest answers, and then report back at a subsequent meeting or retreat. Most boards find that they are strong in some areas and have room for improvement in others.

For the sake of consistency, we use specific terms in these questions that have appeared throughout this book. "Council" refers to the governing board, "overseer" refers to each board member, "ministry" points to the Christ-centered church or nonprofit organization in view, and "administrator" or "administration" refers to the individual steward or the team that manages the day-to-day ministry operations.

Here are the twenty questions. You may come up with others too. We offer them as a map of sorts to help you discern with the Holy Spirit where to go from here.

1. How do the council and the administration each demonstrate and communicate that they are stewards and not owners and that God is the sole owner of the ministry?

2. What intentional actions might both the council and the administration take to help the ministry's constituents trust in God's abundant provision?

3. Can the council and the administration produce a list of faithful practices that ensure that the ministry does what is right before God in their sector of God's work?

4. How do the council and the administration empower ministry staff to engage in God's work by grace and exhibit that they trust God for results in faith?

5. What specific biblical stewardship matters do the council and the administration attend to, on a regular basis, to ensure they preserve God's honor in both what they do and how they do it?

6. Has the ministry joined or maintained an accreditation with a peer accountability group to verify compliance with God-honoring, law-abiding, biblically based standards of responsible stewardship?

7. What practices have the council and the administration put in place to keep obedience to God as a key filter for decision-making and risk management?

8. What qualitative metrics linked to ministry activities do the council and the administration use to show that their efforts aim at advancing God's kingdom rather than merely growing an earthly one?

9. What specific illustrations or applications reveal that the council governs and serves as a Christ-centered body and not as a group of rulers controlling a business?

10. How do the council and administration feed on the Word of God and use it as a filter for making decisions and for finding answers in the face of difficulties?

11. What spiritual oversight activities do the council and the administration engage in to discern direction from the Holy Spirit including having margin for silence to listen?

12. What actions do the council and the administration take to preserve the unity of the Spirit and the bond of peace with each other and with the ministry staff and constituents?

13. What practical steps do the council and the administration take to steward change and to make sure the ministry is working where God is working?

14. What faithful activities and fruit do the council and the administration celebrate with the staff to inspire ongoing fruitful service?

15. Does the council have a selection process that prioritizes candidates for the role of overseer based on Christian maturity and administrative gifting and that protects against scheming and exploitation?

16. Does the composition of the council reflect the diversity and values of the Christ-centered ministry?

17. Does the council evaluate its members so they set an example in speech and conduct, so they are sure to show God's love and uplift those they serve?

18. What practical activities help the council assume a standing rather than a sitting posture in governance so they are positioned to share burdens and serve humbly?

19. How can the ministry's constituents visibly see and approach the council and the administration, so they stay connected with each other in doing God's work?

20. How are the overseers and the administrators encouraged to give cheerfully, serve sacrificially, and pray faithfully as role models of participation in God's work?

We hope these questions prompt rich discussion and help point the way forward for councils all over the world.

Remember to start your journey at Arles. Pick up where exemplary councils of the biblical and historical record left off. Govern in submission to the Holy Spirit and ask hard questions to discern direction. Align your perspective and practices with God's design for governance.

We pray that your oversight reflects the posture of our Lord Jesus Christ, and that the Holy Spirit will lead and guide your council for God's glory.

Study Guide

*"We all want progress. But progress means getting
nearer to the place where you want to be.
And if you have taken a wrong turning,
then to go forward does not get you any nearer.
If you are on the wrong road, progress means doing
an about-turn and walking back to the right road;
in that case, the man who turns back soonest
is the most progressive."*[31]
C.S. Lewis

This study guide seeks to help readers process the biblical material along with our content more deeply. We invite you to read each chapter, explore questions for discussion, meditate on related Scriptures, pray about how God's Spirit may be leading you, and act in obedience by responding to the content.

Chapter One

Read: Chapter 1 – The Council of Moses

Explore: Consider these statements and questions for discussion.

1. Tell the story of Numbers 11 in your own words.

2. Summarize the frustration of Moses (11:11–15). Can you share about a time when you felt similarly exasperated?

3. Why do you think the Lord instructed Moses to locate seventy elders and officials who were known to him (11:16)?

4. Where must the seventy assemble, in what posture, and why do you think the Lord gives these guidelines (11:16–17)?

5. When the Spirit showed up at the tent of meeting and in the camp, what does the response of Joshua as compared to Moses teach us about control versus governance (11:24–30)?

6. The Lord ordered the seventy to help Moses "share the burden of the people" (11:17). What might that look like today?

7. How does the Council of Moses provide a foundational biblical framework for thinking about governance?

Meditate: Reflect on related Scriptures. Exodus 18:19–23, 24:9–11, 31:1–5; and Deuteronomy 1:9–18.

Pray: How do you sense the Holy Spirit speaking to you through reflection on the Council of Moses and governance?

Act: How will the Council of Moses shape your thinking about governance from this point forward?

Chapter Two

Read: Chapter 2 – The Jewish Council in the First Century

Explore: Consider these statements and questions for discussion.

1. What does "Sanhedrin" mean? Compare this group in form and function to the Council of Moses.

2. Describe the four snares of the Sanhedrin in your own words.

3. How did the selection process for the Jewish Council differ from the Council of Moses?

4. What factors reveal the Sanhedrin's shift from governing to ruling and controlling (John 11:47–50)?

5. How does a group of humans who rule rather than govern then fall into the trap of idolatry to money?

6. How might a governing board's posture, language, and proximity to those they serve reflect pride?

7. How does the Sanhedrin inform our biblical perspective for thinking about how not to govern?

Meditate: Reflect on related Scriptures. Matthew 21:12–17, 26:57–59; Mark 11:15–19, 12:38–40, 15:1; Luke 16:13–15, 19:45–48, 20:47, 22:66; John 2:13–1, 3:1, 18:12–13; Acts 4:5–10, 5:27, 23:1–11; Ephesians 5:5; Colossians 3:5; 1 Timothy 3:3; and Titus 1:7.

Pray: How do you sense the Holy Spirit speaking to you through reflection on the Sanhedrin and governance?

Act: How will the Sanhedrin shape your thinking about how not to govern both now and in the future?

Chapter Three

Read: Chapter 3 – The Gentile Councils of the Roman World

Explore: Consider these statements and questions for discussion.

1. Retell the story of the Council of Ephesus (Acts 19:23–41).

2. Describe the four pitfalls of the Council of Ephesus in your own words.

3. How did Rome shape the composition of councils in the cities of the ancient Mediterranean world?

4. What factors gave the city clerk power over the Ephesians, and why did they respond to his rule (Acts 19:35–41)?

5. How do the remarks of Demetrius reveal that money was a bigger idol in Ephesus than Artemis (Acts 19:23–27)?

6. In what ways do Demetrius, the Ephesian crowd, and the city clerk reflect pride related to governance in this story?

7. How does the Council of Ephesus inform our biblical perspective for thinking about how not to govern?

Meditate: Reflect on related Scriptures. Acts 19:1–22, 23:23–35, 24:1–27.

Pray: How do you sense the Holy Spirit speaking to you through reflection on the Council of Ephesus and governance?

Act: How will the Council of Ephesus shape your thinking about how not to govern both now and in the future?

Chapter Four

Read: Chapter 4 - The Jerusalem Council in Acts of the Apostles

Explore: Consider these statements and questions for discussion.

1. Describe the problem that brought the Jerusalem Council together in Acts 15 in your own words.

2. What practical governance insights do you gain by observing how the proceedings transpired in Acts 15?

3. Why do you think the Jerusalem Council only contained "apostles and elders" (Acts 15:6)?

4. What role did the Scriptures play in the Jerusalem Council proceedings, and why is it significant that Amos was quoted from the LXX (Acts 15:13–21)?

5. How does the decision of the Jerusalem Council show that its willingness not to try to control the work of the Holy Spirit as overseers would actually position the church for exponential growth (Acts 15:23–29)?

6. Why do you think the contents and delivery of the letter from the Jerusalem Council would foster unity?

7. How does the Jerusalem Council enrich our biblical perspective for thinking about governance?

Meditate: Reflect on related Scriptures. Amos 9:11–12 (LXX); Matthew 16:18; Acts 2:1–13, 11:18, 11:26.

Pray: How do you sense the Holy Spirit speaking to you through reflection on the Jerusalem Council and governance?

Act: How will the Jerusalem Council shape your thinking about governance from this point forward?

Chapter Five

Read: Chapter 5 – Mindset: A Biblical Framework for Board Governance

Explore: Consider these statements and questions for discussion.

1. In your own words, explain why words like "abstain" and "adopting" strengthen a biblical mindset for governance.

2. Why is it important that a biblical mindset on governance be framed descriptively rather than prescriptively?

3. What dangers should board members avoid and what steps would they do well to take in building a candidate selection process for oversight roles?

4. How can standing and listening to the reading of Scripture shape the mindset of board members toward governing and away from ruling and controlling?

5. How might standards of responsible stewardship help overseers of Christ-centered churches and ministries make

sure the ministries they serve depend on the power of the Holy Spirit rather than money to fuel God's work?

6. How might the rhythms of prayer and fasting, the evaluation of language and perceptions, and peer accountability help overseers root out pride?

7. What facet of this biblical mindset might be most difficult for a governing board to adopt?

Meditate: Reflect on related Scriptures. Jonah 1:4–7; Matthew 4:1–11, 6:5–18, 24, 7:21–23, 16:18, 23, 16:25:14–30; Luke 10:1–12, 19:11–27; John 13:29; Acts 1:21–26, 4:11–21, 4:32–37, 6:1–7, 8:18–24, 13:1–3, 14:23, 15:20; Romans 15:25–29 (NASB); 1 Corinthians 1:26–31; 1 Timothy 3:1–7; Titus 1:5–10; James 1:19–25; 1 Peter 5:1–5.

Pray: How do you sense the Holy Spirit speaking to you through reflection on this biblical mindset?

Act: How will this biblical mindset shape your thinking about governance from this point forward?

Chapter Six

Read: Chapter 6 – Model: Maintaining a Biblical Mindset on Board Governance

Explore: Consider these statements and questions for discussion.

1. What's significant about the fact that numerous councils in the early church after the Jerusalem Council adopted the "formula" of Acts 15:28?

2. What four formational disciplines come together to provide a model for helping boards maintain a biblical mindset?

3. List various benefits that can come to boards that make Scripture reading a key part of their regular proceedings.

4. How might your board include extended times of silence to attune to the Holy Spirit with regard to governance?

5. What might need to change in your board agenda so everyone has a voice and remains engaged?

6. What does supplication look like for your board and what does it reflect regarding dependency upon God?

7. What discipline of this biblical model might be most difficult for a governing board to practice?

Meditate: Reflect on related Scriptures. Psalm 46:10; Jeremiah 3:15; Matthew 14:13; Mark 1:35; Philippians 4:6–7; 2 Timothy 3:16–17; James 1:19.

Pray: How do you sense the Holy Spirit speaking to you through reflection on this biblical model?

Act: How will this biblical model shape your governance practices from this point forward?

Chapter Seven

Read: Chapter 7 – Map: Return to Arles and Ask Hard Questions

Explore: Consider these statements and questions for discussion.

1. In your own words, explain the call to "Return to Arles" in the context of governance.

2. What intentional disciplines could your board practice to demonstrate submission to the leading and guidance of the Holy Spirit?

3. If you put a copy of the print *Café Terrace at Night* in your boardroom, what impact might it have on your governing board?

4. In your own words, explain the value and importance of the twenty hard questions for helping boards align with a biblical perspective.

5. Which of the twenty hard questions might be the most difficult for your board to address?

6. Which of the twenty hard questions might be the most difficult for your administrators to address?

7. How do you believe the exhortations to "Return to Arles" and "Ask Hard Questions" will impact your board moving forward?

Meditate: Reflect on related Scriptures. Psalm 51; Proverbs 28:13; John 5:30; Galatians 5:16-26; Ephesians 4:2; James 4:8-10.

Pray: How do you sense the Holy Spirit speaking to you through reflection on the biblical perspective outlined in this book?

Act: How will you help your board "Return to Arles" and "Ask Hard Questions" from this point forward?

Endnotes

[1] Ronald B. Allen, *Expositor's Bible Commentary 2: Numbers*, ed. Frank Gaebelein, (Grand Rapids, MI: Zondervan, 1990), 794.

[2] Gordon Wenham, *Tyndale Old Testament Commentaries 4: Numbers*, (Downers Grove, IL: IVP Academic, 2008), 122.

[3] Two resources expand brilliantly on this topic outside the bounds of this study: R. Scott Rodin, *The Steward Leader: Transforming People, Organizations and Communities* (Downers Grove, IL: IVP Academic, 2010); and, Kent R. Wilson, *Steward Leadership in the Nonprofit Organization* (Downers Grove, IL: IVP, 2016).

[4] Graham H. Twelftree, "Sanhedrin," in *Dictionary of Jesus in the Gospels*, eds. Joel B. Green, Scot McKnight, and I. Howard Marshall (Downers Grove, IL: IVP, 1992), 731.

[5] Gary M. Burge, *The New Testament in Antiquity: A Survey of the New Testament within its Cultural Contexts*, Chapter 3, "The World of Jesus in His Jewish Homeland" (Grand Rapids, MI: Zondervan, 2009), 70.

[6] Graham H. Twelftree, "Sanhedrin," 730.

[7] For further reading on this point, see: Gary G. Hoag, R. Scott Rodin, and Wesley K. Willmer, *The Choice: The Christ-Centered Pursuit of Kingdom Outcomes* (Winchester, VA: ECFA Press, 2014), 18-21.

[8] We advise governing boards to adopt the "Biblical Principles for Stewardship and Fundraising" to guide organizational efforts and avoid the snare of idolatry to money. Find them here: R. Scott Rodin and Gary G. Hoag, *The Sower: Redefining the Ministry of Raising Kingdom Resources* (Winchester, VA: ECFA Press, 2010), 81-83.

[9] Jerome Murphy O'Connor, *St. Paul's Ephesus: Texts and Archaeology* (Collegeville, MN: Liturgical Press, 2008), 34.

[10] F.F. Bruce, *New International Commentary on the New Testament: The Book of the Acts*, revised (Grand Rapids, MI: Eerdmans, 1988), 378.

[11] Ben Witherington, III, *The Acts of the Apostles: A Socio-Rhetorical Commentary* (Grand Rapids, MI: Eerdmans, 1998), 439.

[12] David A. DeSilva, *An Introduction to the New Testament: Contexts, Methods, and Ministry Formation* (Downers Grove, IL: IVP Academic, 2004), 381-382.

[13] Michael Horton, *Rediscovering the Holy Spirit: God's Perfecting Presence in Creation, Redemption, and Everyday Life* (Grand Rapids, MI: Zondervan, 2017), 142.

[14] Charles Joseph Hefele, *A History of the Christian Councils: From the Original Documents to the Close of the Council of Nicea, A.D. 325* (Edinburgh, Scotland: T&T Clark, 1871), 1-2.

[15] John R. W. Stott, *The Message of Acts*, TBST (Downers Grove, IL: IVP, 1990), 250.

[16] For examples that provide practical applications in the American context, see: Dan Busby and John Pearson, *Lessons from the Church Boardroom* (Winchester, VA: ECFAPress, 2018); Dan Busby and John Pearson, *Lessons from the Nonprofit Boardroom* (Winchester, VA: ECFAPress, 2017); and, David L. McKenna, *Call of the Chair: Leading the Board of the Christ-Centered Ministry* (Winchester, VA: ECFAPress, 2017). See also the ECFA *Governance Toolbox Series* at: www.ecfa.org/ToolboxSeries.aspx. Accessed on 24 June 2018.

[17] To watch a two-minute video that describes "the Kingdom path" visit: www.thekingdompath.com. Accessed on 18 June 2018.

[18] To read about more about the two paths presented on this chart, see: Gary G. Hoag, R. Scott Rodin, Wesley K. Willmer, *The Choice: The Christ-Centered Pursuit of Kingdom Outcomes* (Winchester, VA: ECFAPress, 2014), 1-13.

[19] Visit www.ecfa.org/Content/Standards to read "ECFA's Seven Standards of Responsible Stewardship™" and commentary associated with each standard. Accessed on 24 June 2018.

[20] For examples of standards adopted by peer accountability groups around the world, visit: www.afcaa.org (African Council for Accreditation and Accountability, Kenya serving pan-Africa), www.cccc.org (Canadian

Council of Christian Charities), www.ccfk.or.kr (Christian Council for Financial Transparency, Korea), www.cctaspace.com (Christian Council for Transparency and Accountability, Philippines), www.cmasc.net.au (Christian Ministry Advancement) Standards Council, Australia), www.efacindia.com (Evangelical Financial Accountability Council, India). Accessed on 24 June 2018.

[21] Charles Joseph Hefele, *A History of the Christian Councils*, 52-53.

[22] Harold M. Daniels, *To God Alone be Glory: The Story and Sources of the Book of Common Worship* (Louisville, KY: Geneva, 2003), 11.

[23] John Cassian (c. 360-435) recounts in his *Institutes and Conferences* that practicing the divine hours dates back to the desert fathers of the third century. More recently, see this helpful book: Phyllis Tickle, *The Divine Hours*, Pocket Edition (Oxford: Oxford University Press, 2007). The divine hours vary based on what sources you view. We suggest this schedule: Lauds or Morning Prayer (6:00 a.m.), Terce or the Morning Office (9:00 a.m.), Sext or the Midday Office (12:00 p.m.), None or Mid-Afternoon Prayer (3:00 p.m.), Vespers or Evening Prayer (6:00 p.m.), Compline or Night Prayer (9:00 p.m.), and Matins or Nocturnes or Night Vigils (12:00 a.m.). Adding the divine hours to your board retreat or to a timeframe leading up at a board meeting with specific Psalms identified for each of the hours can knit the hearts of the board together with each other and God.

[24] Richard J. Foster, *Freedom of Simplicity: Finding Harmony in a Complex World* (New York, NY: HarperCollins, 1981), 72.

[25] Billy Graham, *The Secret of Happiness* (Nashville, TN: Thomas Nelson, 1985), 36-37.

[26] Hudson Taylor in *The Prayer Motivator*, comp. and ed. by Daniel Whyte III (Dallas, TX: Torch Legacy, 2010), 91.

[27] Adoniram Judson, *The American Baptist Magazine and Missionary Intelligencer, Vol. 1.* (Boston, MA: LLE, 1817), 99.

[28] David Bartlett and Paul Campey, *Community Governance: A Framework for Building Healthy Christian Organizations* (Gosford, Australia: Resolve Consulting Group, 2008), 9-10.

[29] John Hardouin, *Conciliorum Collectio Regis Maxima* (Paris: P. Labbei et P. Gabrielis Cossarti, 1715), 262, as cited by Charles Joseph Hefele, *A History of the Christian Councils*, 2.

[30] Todd Van Luling, "Vincent Van Gogh May Have Hidden 'The Last Supper' Within One Of His Most Famous Paintings," published on March 6, 2015. Updated on December 6, 2017. Accessed on June 22, 2018: https://www.huffingtonpost.com /2015/03/06/van-gogh-last-supper_n_6753294.html.

[31] C.S. Lewis, *Mere Christianity* (New York: HarperCollins, 1980), 28.

The Authors

Gary G. Hoag, Ph.D. (New Testament – Trinity College, Bristol, UK) is a passionate follower of Jesus Christ known widely as the Generosity Monk. He posts daily meditations and has written or contributed to ten books. He speaks all over the world bringing a biblical perspective to a wide range of topics. He provides spiritual and strategic counsel for church and nonprofit workers. He serves as a visiting professor at six seminaries in three countries. In collaboration with ECFA, he helps nationals champion the faithful administration and governance of God's work globally. Formerly, he held administrative roles at Biola University, Colorado Christian University, and Denver Seminary, and board positions with four nonprofit organizations. Currently, he serves on two ministry boards. He is married to Jenni, and they have a grown son and daughter, Sammy and Sophie.

Wesley K. Willmer, Ph.D., principal, Wes Willmer Group, LLC, is approaching five decades of service with Christian ministries. Wes has initiated and directed more than $1 million in research grants to study nonprofit leadership. He has been the author, co-author, editor, or editor-in-chief of 25 books and many professional journal articles and publications. He has held executive leadership positions at Wheaton College (IL), Seattle Pacific

University, Prison Fellowship, Biola University, Mission Increase Foundation, Roberts Wesleyan College, and ECFA. His board involvement includes chair of the board of the Christian Stewardship Association (CSA), founding member of the Council for Advancement and Support of Education (CASE) Commission on Philanthropy, vice chair of the Evangelical Council for Financial Accountability (ECFA) board, founding board member and executive committee member of the Christian Leadership Alliance (CLA), and consultant to other boards. He is married to Sharon, and they are blessed with three grown children and seven grandchildren.

 Gregory J. Henson, M.B.A., is deeply committed to the local church and her participation in the work God is doing. Currently, he serves as President at Sioux Falls Seminary, where he has worked with his team to develop revolutionary approaches to financial, educational, and governance models within theological education. As a published author and speaker on the topics of theological education, innovation, generational theory, missional theology, and competency-based education, Greg helps people see the unique opportunities that exist within the challenges they encounter. Prior to serving at Sioux Falls Seminary, Greg served in roles ranging from Vice President of Institutional Advancement to Lead Pastor to Worship Pastor and several more. At the heart of his ministry is a desire to develop kingdom-minded servants for participation in God's Kingdom mission. He is married to Heather, and they have four children.

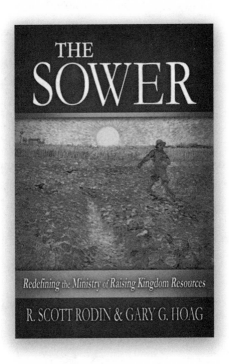

The purpose of this book is to provide momentum to a movement aimed at the heart of every person who is involved in the process of raising money or giving money for the work of God's Kingdom. You may be a full-time development officer, an executive director, a pastor, a president, a board member, a volunteer or a faithful giver. You may have decades of experience in fund development, or this may be the first exposure to this topic. If you care about giving or raising money for God's work, this book is for you.

**Place your order at
ECFA.org/ECFAPress**

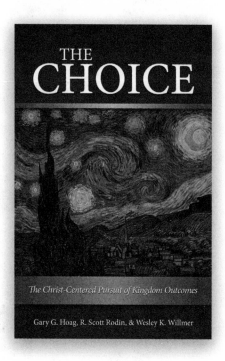

THE CHOICE

The Christ-Centered Pursuit of Kingdom Outcomes

Gary G. Hoag, R. Scott Rodin, & Wesley K. Willmer

There is the continual push for higher and greater results. When we idolize results that we think please Him, we actually fail to exhibit the obedience He asks of us.

So what should ministry look like? Jesus instructs us to follow Him. This is the Kingdom path.

If this sounds oversimplified, we think we are the ones who have complicated things. Jesus recruited ordinary, mostly uneducated people and gave them basic instructions. He used words like "follow," "trust," and "obey." When we pursue the Kingdom path, then fruitfulness is the by-product. The Kingdom path is the only path that leads to Kingdom outcomes.

**Place your order at
ECFA.org/ECFAPress**

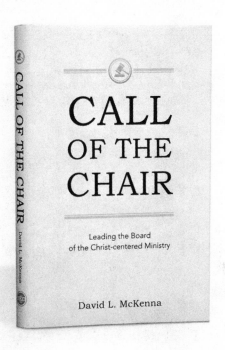

As Christ-centered ministries go through changing times, the leadership role of the board chair rises in significance. As manager of the board, the chair joins the CEO in responsibility for advancing the mission, partnering with the vision, governing by policy, and setting the tone for the morale of the ministry. Such leadership requires a chair who is appointed by God, gifted with integrity, trust and humility, and anointed by the Holy Spirit.

With deft strokes written out of learning from professional practice, understanding from spiritual discipline, and insight from personal experience, David McKenna leaves no doubt. Unless chosen by God, the chair will fail; unless gifted with integrity, trust and humility, the board will fail; and unless obedient to the Spirit, the ministry will fail. Loud and clear, the message is sent to every Christ-centered ministry: The call of the chair is the call of God.

**Place your order at
ECFA.org/ECFAPress**

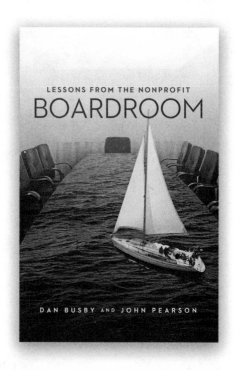

This book is based on the wisdom and experience of two seasoned veterans in the Christ-centered nonprofit arena. Written in an engaging, easy-to-read and understandable style, the authors provide 40 short lessons for inspiring your board in God-honoring governance. The lessons are ideal for use in board training.

Each short lesson raises an issue, offers insight, and then proposes specific action steps. Topics include:

- What to do *before* the meeting
- How (and why) to create a Board Policies Manual
- How to listen to the Holy Spirit
- How an effective board chair functions best

Check out the *Lessons From the Nonprofit Boardroom* blog: *https://nonprofitboardroom.blogspot.com/*.

**Place your order at
ECFA.org/ECFAPress**

LESSONS FROM THE CHURCH
BOARDROOM

DAN BUSBY & JOHN PEARSON

You will feel like *Lessons From the Church Boardroom* is describing many of the church board meetings that you have attended.

Disarming yet authoritative, enjoyable yet challenging, the authors quickly pinpoint a challenging situation and then show you a better way to handle it. Your future service on church boards will never be the same after reading this book. You will gain many great ideas for building trust and increasing effectiveness whether as a church board leader or member.

You'll laugh and relate to painful moments, but most of all you'll walk away better equipped for your board's vital role in tackling your church's God-given mission.

Check out the *Lessons From the Church Boardroom* blog: *https://churchboardroom.blogspot.com/*.

**Place your order at
ECFA.org/ECFAPress**